THE BRADLEY SMOKER COOKBOOK

THE BRADLEY SMOKER COOKBOOK

Tips, Tricks, and Recipes from Bradley Smoker's Pro Staff

LENA CLAYTON, STEVE CYLKA, KATHLEEN DONEGAN, BRAD LOCKWOOD, AND JENNIFER L. S. PEARSALL

Skyhorse Publishing

Skyhorse Publishing books may be purchased in bulk at special discounts for sales promotion, corporate gifts, fund-raising, or educational purposes. Special editions can also be created to specifications. For details, contact the Special Sales Department, Skyhorse Publishing, 307 West 36th Street, 11th Floor, New York, NY 10018 or info@skyhorsepublishing.com.

Skyhorse® and Skyhorse Publishing® are registered trademarks of Skyhorse Publishing, Inc.®, a Delaware corporation.

Visit our website at www.skyhorsepublishing.com.

10 9 8

Library of Congress Cataloging-in-Publication Data is available on file.

Cover design by Brian Peterson
Cover photo credit Bradley Smoker, Inc.

Print ISBN: 978-1-63220-715-9
Ebook ISBN: 978-1-63220-793-7

Printed in China

CONTENTS

Introduction 1

The Writers 3

Bradley Bisquette Flavor Guide 8

Lena Clayton 9

Smoked Sweet Chili Nuts 11

Smoked Corn Salsa 13

Smoked Tomato and Herb Soup 15

Watercress and Smoked Pear Salad 17

Smoked Duck and Fig Salad 19

Smoked Tuna and Avocado Salad 21

Smoked Salmon Puff Pastries 22

Mackerel Smørrebrød (Danish Open-Faced Sandwich) 25

Bacon and Smoked Mushroom Linguine 27

Soba Noodle Salad with Asian Smoked Duck 29

Chardonnay Marinated Salmon with Creamy Dill-Cucumber Sauce 31

Smoked Bison Burgers 32

Smoked Chocolate Bacon Truffles 34

Smoked Sea Salt Caramels 37

Smoked Peach Cobbler 38

Brad Lockwood 41

Jalapeño and Cheese Bear Bratwurst 43

Elk Summer Sausage 45

Ground Moose Jerky 47

Hickory Smoked Turkey Bacon 49

Mesquite Smoked Cracked Pepper and Garlic Venison Snack Sticks 51

Polish Venison Smoked Sausage 53

Smoked Venison Ham 55

Whole Muscle Turkey Jerky 57

Wild Boar Hot Sausage 59

Steve Cylka **61**

Cajun Smoked Catfish 63

Cherrywood Smoked Double Garlic Kielbasa 65

Maple Smoked Bacon 67

Competition Smoked BBQ Ribs 69

Smoked Buffalo Chicken Wings 71

Bacon Wrapped Chicken Breast Stuffed with Spinach and Cheese 73

Smoked Chipotle Maple Chicken Salad 75

Smoked Meatloaf with Bacon Weave Wrap 77

Smoked Salmon Nuggets with Maple Cream Dip 79

Smoked Shrimp Risotto 81

Steve's Smoked Tomato Soup 83

Pasta with Smoked Pork Tenderloin and Tomato Basil Cream Sauce 85

Smoked Cheese 87

Smoked Maple Beans 89

Smoked Pulled Pork 91

Dragon Jalapeño Poppers 93

Kathleen Donegan **95**

Applewood Smoked Fusion Turkey Breast with Cilantro-Lime Mayonnaise 97

One-Pound Pork Tenderloin with Asian Rub and Cucumber Salad 98

Mixed Smoked Vegetable Tray 100

Mustard Smoked Rack of Lamb 103

Peaches Smoked with Brown Sugar and Bourbon 105

Smoked Pickled Green Beans 107

Smoked Sea Scallops with Arugula Salad 109

Smoked Silver Trout Spread 111

Smoked Stuffed Tomatoes 113

Smoked Turkey Pastrami 115

Smoked Bluefish 116

Smoked Cream of Tomato Soup 119

Smoked Mussels with Zucchini Relish 121

Berbere Pork Belly for Dinner 123

Spicy Smoked Shrimp 125

Three Smoked Cheeses 127

Jennifer L. S. Pearsall **129**

Smoked Apple Slaw and Pork Shoulder Sliders 130

Smoked Asian Burger..133

Bacon-Wrapped Smoked Brown Sugar Onion Rings 135

Smoked Buffalo Chicken Pot Pie...136

Smoked Cream of Mushroom and Red Bell Pepper Soup...139

Smoked Greek Chicken Gyros..141

Smoked Outside-In All-American Burger 143

Smoked Pepper Relish 145

Smoked Pulled Pork, Wild Rice, and Cabbage Pie..146

Smoked Salmon Inverted Samosas..149

Smoked Sausage and Mozzarella Bites 151

Smoked Scotched Eggs 153

Smoked Spiced Pork Tenderloin with Smoked Plum Sauce..155

Smoked Stuffed Italian Burger 157

Smoked Summer Chowder 158

Smoked Onion and Bacon Jam..161

Bradley Smoker Tips and Tricks...**163**

INTRODUCTION

Another cookbook, eh? First and foremost, I want to thank everyone who contributed to this book's creation. The collaboration and willingness to bring it all together is greatly appreciated.

At Bradley, we have a very simple philosophy behind smoked food and what it takes to make smoked food taste great. By using as little heat as possible to make wood smoke, never allowing the wood to burn completely down to ash, and controlling your heat, your food will have that rich, clean smoke flavor. That's it—simple, eh? If you have not guessed it, I am Canadian, and yes, we do know a thing or two about smoking and preserving food.

Since we got into this business, we have enjoyed learning how to make bacon, pulled pork, jerkies, game sausages, and many more smoked food specialties. Back in the '70s, my dad used to make smoked salmon with an exceptional recipe. We still make it during the holiday season every year. Back then, he used a large bread oven and a frying pan full of sawdust that he tended to about every half hour. He used nothing but alder wood sawdust and would dump the spent sawdust into a waste bin, replacing it with fresh sawdust in the frying pan. He would smoke about twenty large fillets of salmon at a time, and the process usually took about twenty turns and lasted ten to twelve hours. During these long periods of watching his fish smoke, he came up with the idea that is a Bradley Smoker today: an automatic smoke generating system built around a simple philosophy about food smoking. There were hundreds of people who enjoyed that smoked salmon and thousands more who will enjoy what you create with the Bradley Smoker today. Thanks Dad!

Personally, I sincerely hope you enjoy this book and the recipes from these fine chefs and gourmet professionals. The only advice I can add is to give yourself lots of time to prepare and smoke your fine foods. There is nothing rushed about food smoking. I find this to be a good thing, as I am usually enjoying the company of friends and family while I am smoking the next meal.

Yours truly,
Wade Bradley

THE WRITERS

LENA CLAYTON (VANCOUVER, BC, CANADA)

Lena Clayton began cooking from a young age and was hooked from the start. She has worked in kitchens of various restaurants, and all that experience has culminated to where she is today, one of the co-owners of a full-service restaurant and catering business in Vancouver, BC. Lena was introduced to smoked foods early on through traditional Danish cooking at home. Throughout Scandinavia, smoking is a common culinary preparation method rooted in traditional food preservation, which is used mainly on fish and pork. Lena's interest in smoking developed as she wished to see how to take this technique further to use it outside of and beyond its traditional form. Drawing from flavors from around the world, Lena cooks to make smoked food accessible to all.

BRAD LOCKWOOD (BROOKVILLE, PENNSYLVANIA, USA)

Brad has been a commercial meat processor for the past twenty-five years and is a previous President of the Pennsylvania Association of Meat Processors. He is the current host of *Love of the Hunt TV,* which airs nationally, as well as in Canada. He is also the producer of Outdoor Edge's complete series of *Wild Game Processing* DVDs. Brad is the host of multiple game processing blogs and forum sites and is a renowned seminar speaker.

STEVE CYLKA (TORONTO, ONTARIO, CANADA)

Steve is a recipe developer, food photographer, and brand ambassador. He is the author of *The Black Peppercorn,* a website featuring original recipes he has created and photographed. Along with his website, he is also a freelance blogger and competes in various culinary competitions. In 2012, he won the Courvoisier Collective Culinary Masterpiece Competition. Having lived in both rural Ontario and Toronto, Steve has an understanding of cooking down home country food, as well as upscale fine dining cuisine. While versatile in the kitchen, Steve specializes in grilling, modernist cuisine, and especially smoking. As the proud owner of a Bradley Smoker for many years, Steve has used it to produce some incredible BBQ dishes. Steve is known for curing and smoking his own bacon, kielbasa, and andouille sausage and gifting them to friends and family. Some of his favorite things to make in the smoker are BBQ ribs, atomic buffalo turds, smoked meatloaf, and pulled pork.

KATHLEEN DONEGAN (PHILADELPHIA, PENNSYLVANIA, USA)

Kathleen Donegan has had a long obsession with the impact food can have on our health, behavior, and general well-being. The problems of hunger and fair distribution of good food in America are driving forces for her. Kathleen is lucky to be surrounded by lots of fabulous farmers and producers in Philadelphia, but even with all of this bounty, she still sees folks eating processed, factory-produced food and fast food as the basis of their diets. She wants to share with people that it is not hard to eat locally and seasonally and to eat food that is humanely raised and chemical free. When someone tells her that they are going to the farmers' markets and are shopping for humanely-raised meats and poultry or, even better, that they are scratch cooking and avoiding take out, she feels totally validated and that is exactly what she wants her blog, *The Philly Foodist,* to accomplish.

JENNIFER L. S. PEARSALL

Jennifer L. S. Pearsall has been a freelance writer, editor, and photographer in the outdoor industry for more than twenty years. Her byline has appeared in dozens of outdoor and sporting magazines since the late 1990s, and she is the author of the *Big Book of Bacon*, as well as a second cookbook to be released with Skyhorse Publishing in late 2015. She currently works as the Director of Public Relations with a nonprofit trade organization in Connecticut, where she resides with her two Great Pyrenees dogs, Lucy and Hayden, who eat bacon every chance they get.

BRADLEY BISQUETTE FLAVOR GUIDE

Bradley Bisquette Food Smoking Guide

	Description	Poultry	Fish & Seafood	Beef	Pork	Lamb	Game	Water Fowl	Vegetables	Nuts	Cheese
Alder	Smooth, delicate, slightly sweet, woody flavor	✓	✓		✓						
Apple	Light, sweet, delicate, and fruity flavor	✓		✓	✓	✓					✓
Cherry	Sweet, delicate flavor	✓	✓	✓	✓	✓		✓	✓		✓
Hickory	Strong, hearty, smoky flavor	✓		✓	✓		✓	✓		✓	✓
Jim Beam	Strong, rich flavor made from the oak barrels of Jim Beam bourbon			✓	✓	✓	✓	✓			
Maple	Sweet, subtle flavor	✓	✓		✓				✓		✓
Mesquite	Strong but sweeter and more delicate than hickory			✓	✓		✓	✓		✓	
Oak	Assertive and versatile	✓		✓	✓	✓	✓				
Pacific Blend	Light and clean flavor	✓	✓						✓		✓
Pecan	Similar to hickory but more subtle	✓		✓	✓	✓	✓	✓			
Special Blend	Distinct but mild	✓	✓	✓	✓	✓					
Whiskey Oak	Strong, rich flavor made from oak whiskey barrels	✓		✓	✓	✓	✓	✓			

For recipes and inspiration, visit www.bradleysmoker.com

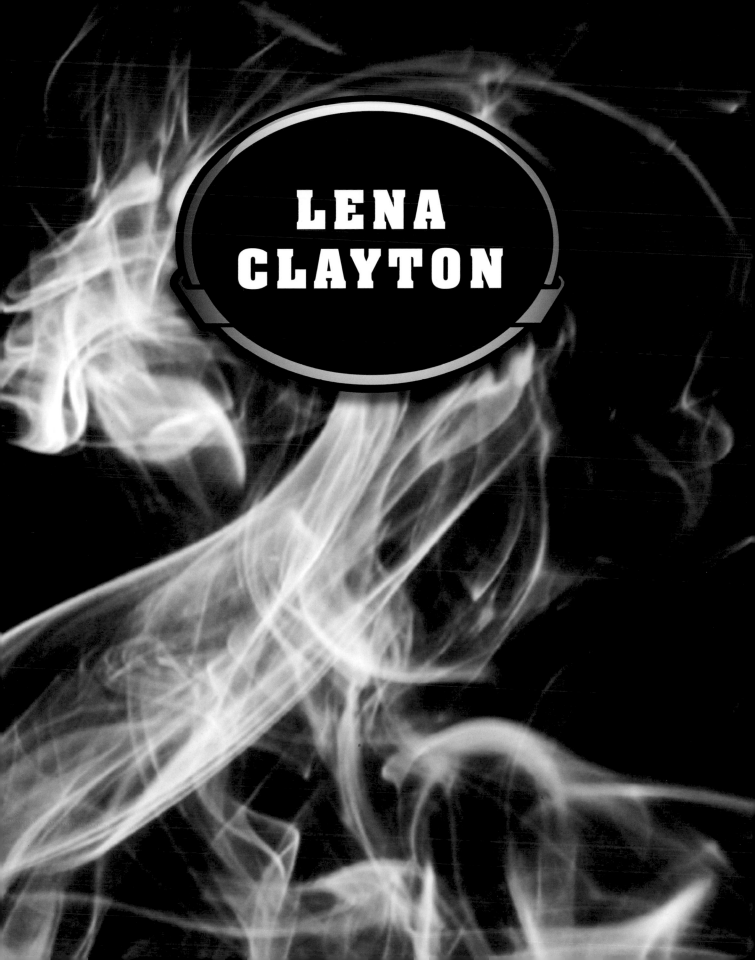

Smoked Sweet Chili Nuts

Makes 2½ cups

Sweet, spicy, and smoky nuts. Great for snacking and for parties.

Ingredients
- 2 cups raw mixed nuts (cashews, almonds, pecans, walnuts, or peanuts will all work well)
- ½ cup shredded coconut
- 2 Tbsp butter
- 3 Tbsp honey
- 1 Tbsp brown sugar
- 1 tsp Sambal Oelek or other chili sauce
- Pinch salt

Directions
1. Soak raw nuts in warm water for 10 minutes.
2. Drain water and place nuts in an aluminum pan with holes punctured in the base.
3. Smoke nuts with Hickory Bisquettes for 3 hours at 194°F (90°C), stirring frequently.
4. Preheat oven to 350°F.
5. Melt butter in a saucepan and remove from heat.
6. Stir in honey, brown sugar, chili sauce, and salt.
7. Transfer smoked nuts to a bowl, mix in shredded coconut, and pour butter-sugar mixture over.
8. Toss nuts in butter-sugar mixture until evenly coated.
9. Pour coated nuts onto a baking sheet prepared with parchment paper.
10. Bake for 20 minutes, stirring every 5 minutes.
11. Allow nuts to cool to room temperature before serving.

Smoked Corn Salsa

Makes 2–3 cups

Fresh salsa with an earthy smoke flavor from the whole smoked corn.

Ingredients
- 2 ears of corn
- 2 medium-sized tomatoes
- ¼ of a medium-sized onion
- 1–3 tsp jalapeño, minced (depending on how spicy you want it to be)
- 1 Tbsp fresh lime juice
- 3 Tbsp fresh cilantro, chopped
- 1 tsp salt
- ½ tsp black pepper

Directions
1. Remove husk and silk from corn.
2. Smoke corn for 2 hours with Hickory Bisquettes at 212–248°F (100–120°C).
3. Once corn is cool enough to handle, cut kernels off the cob.
4. Core, seed, and dice tomatoes.
5. Dice onion.
6. Combine smoked corn kernels, diced tomatoes, diced onion, minced jalapeño, lime juice, chopped cilantro, salt, and pepper in a bowl.

Smoked Tomato and Herb Soup

Makes 2 servings

Rich and flavorful tomatoes smoked and puréed with fresh herbs.

Ingredients
- 6 large tomatoes
- 1 Tbsp olive oil
- ½ medium-sized onion, sliced
- 4 garlic cloves, minced
- 1 Tbsp fresh rosemary, chopped
- 2 Tbsp fresh basil, chopped
- 2 Tbsp parsley, chopped
- Salt and pepper

Directions
1. Cut tomatoes into segments, remove seeds, and core.
2. Place tomatoes in aluminum trays and smoke with Hickory Bisquettes for 3 hours at 194°F (90°C).
3. Heat oil in a medium-sized pot, add onions and garlic.
4. Cook over medium heat while stirring constantly until lightly browned, 3–5 minutes.
5. Add smoked tomatoes and their juices to the pot.
6. Cook covered for 15 minutes.
7. Transfer cooked tomatoes, onions, and garlic into a heatproof blender and blend.
8. Return blended soup to the pot and season to taste with salt and pepper.
9. Stir in fresh herbs and serve hot.

Watercress and Smoked Pear Salad

Makes 4 servings

Bitter watercress with smoky and sweet pears, fragrant blue cheese, and toasted pecans dressed in a maple vinaigrette.

Ingredients
- 1 bunch watercress
- 2 pears (a firm varietal such as Anjou)
- ½ cup pecans
- 50 g (3 Tbsp) Danish blue cheese

For Maple Vinaigrette
- ¼ cup canola oil
- ¼ cup apple cider vinegar
- ⅛ cup maple syrup

Directions
1. Cut pears in half and remove stems and cores.
2. Smoke pears in an aluminum tray on the lowest setting, aiming for 104°F (40°C), for 1 hour with Maple Bisquettes and an aluminum tray filled with ice on the rack underneath the pears to help regulate the temperature.
3. Toast pecans on a baking tray for 7–8 minutes at 350°F.
4. Pluck groups of watercress leaves off larger stems and wash well.
5. Whisk together ingredients for maple vinaigrette.
6. Once pears have cooled, slice into wedges.
7. Mix together all salad ingredients and dress with desired amount of maple vinaigrette.

Smoked Duck and Fig Salad

Makes 4 servings

Tender duck breast, peppery arugula, fresh figs, and herbs dressed in a red wine vinaigrette.

Ingredients

For 80% Brine
- 211 g (¾ cup) salt
- 1 L water

For Red Wine Vinaigrette
- ½ cup vegetable oil
- ½ cup red wine vinegar
- 1½ Tbsp honey
- Pinch salt
- ¼ tsp white pepper

For Salad
- 2 duck breasts
- 250 g (8 cups) baby arugula
- 4 fresh figs, quartered
- 6–7 basil leaves, chiffonade
- 2 Tbsp chives, chopped

Directions
1. Dissolve salt in water to create 80% brine solution.
2. Brine both duck breasts overnight in solution.
3. Score skin side of breasts with a paring knife, being careful not to pierce through flesh and only cut the fat cap.
4. Smoke duck breasts with Oak Bisquettes at 212°F (100°C) for 1–2 hours until an internal temperature of 158°F (70°C) is reached.
5. Remove from smoker and let rest at room temperature.
6. Whisk together ingredients for vinaigrette.
7. When duck has cooled enough to handle, slice into thin strips.
8. Arrange salad ingredients over arugula and dress with desired amount of vinaigrette.

Smoked Tuna and Avocado Salad

Makes 2 servings

Soy marinated Albacore tuna loin lightly smoked, served with diced avocado, and tossed in a chili and lime dressing.

Ingredients
- Albacore tuna loin
- 2 avocados, cut into 1 cm cubes
- 1 green onion, thinly sliced
- 1 Tbsp sesame seeds

For Marinade
- ¼ cup brown sugar
- 2 Tbsp salt
- 1 Tbsp soy sauce
- 2 cups water

For Dressing
- 3 Tbsp lime juice
- 2 tsp soy sauce
- 1 tsp Sambal Oelek

Directions
1. Whisk together marinade ingredients.
2. Cut tuna loin into 3–4 cm long segments and submerge in marinade, soak for 20 minutes.
3. Remove from marinade and place cut loin in foil trays.
4. Smoke with Hickory Bisquettes for 45 minutes at 140°F (60°C).
5. Cut tuna into 1 cm cubes and refrigerate immediately.
6. Whisk together ingredients for dressing.
7. Once tuna is fully cooled, combine with avocado.
8. Toss tuna and avocado in dressing.
9. Garnish with green onions and sesame seeds.

Smoked Salmon Puff Pastries

Makes 4 servings

A breakfast pastry made of flaky dough filled with smoked salmon, potatoes, peas, capers, and herbs.

Ingredients

- 150 g (2 cups) white potato
- 1 tsp salt
- 1 Tbsp butter
- 400 g (0.88 lb) frozen puff pastry

For Filling

- 100 g (0.22 lb) smoked salmon, as per your favourite recipe
- 1 Tbsp parsley

- 1 tsp lemon zest
- 1 Tbsp capers
- ¼ cup red onion, minced
- ¼ cup frozen peas
- Salt and pepper to season

For Egg Wash

- 1 egg
- 1 Tbsp water

Directions

1. Thaw pastry as per package direction.
2. Cut potatoes into 2–3 cm cubes.
3. Place in a small saucepan and fill with enough water to cover all the potatoes with 3 cm of water.
4. Add 1 tsp of salt and bring pot to a boil over medium-high heat.
5. Reduce heat to medium and simmer for 10–15 minutes or until tender.
6. Remove from heat, drain, and rinse potatoes under cold water.
7. Roughly mash potatoes with 1 Tbsp butter.
8. Mix remaining filling ingredients in with potatoes and season to taste.
9. Roll out thawed pastry in a rectangle 1 cm thick.
10. Cut pastry into 6 squares, each approximately 10 cm by 10 cm.
11. Add approximately ¼ cup of filling rolled into a ball to the center of each pastry square.
12. Fold the corners of each square toward the center and pinch together edges to seal filling inside the pastry. Wetting your fingers with water will help to ensure a proper seal.
13. Place all sealed pastries into the fridge for 30 minutes, which will cool the butter in the pastry to help make it flaky.
14. Preheat oven to 350°F.
15. Whisk together egg and water.
16. Place all pastries seamed-side down on a baking tray lined with parchment paper.
17. Lightly brush outside of pastries with egg wash.
18. Bake in preheated oven for 20 minutes or until golden brown.

Mackerel Smørrebrød (Danish Open-Faced Sandwich)

Makes 4 servings

A traditional Danish open-faced sandwich with rich smoked mackerel, dill mayonnaise, and a fresh apple slaw.

Ingredients

- 1 whole mackerel, scaled, gutted, and deboned
- 8 slices of Scandinavian-style rye bread

For 80% Brine
- 53 g (3 Tbsp) salt
- 250 mL water

For Slaw
- 1 green apple
- Juice from ½ a lemon

- 1 cup water
- ¼ red onion, thinly sliced
- 2 Tbsp fresh parsley, chopped
- 2 tsp apple cider vinegar
- ¼ tsp salt
- ¼ tsp pepper

For Dill Mayonnaise
- 3 Tbsp mayonnaise
- 1 Tbsp fresh dill, minced

Directions

1. Whisk together salt and water for 80% brine solution.
2. Submerge mackerel in 80% brine solution for 10 minutes.
3. Smoke mackerel skin side down with Pacific Blend Bisquettes for 1 hour at 149°F (65°C) or until an internal temperature of 122°F (50°C) is reached.
4. Increase heat to 194°F (90°C) and smoke for another hour or until an internal temperature of 158°F (70°C) is reached.
5. Whisk together lemon juice and water in a bowl.
6. Julienne apple and submerge into lemon water for 5 minutes.
7. Remove apple from lemon water and place in a bowl.
8. Add sliced red onion and parsley and mix.
9. Dress slaw with apple cider vinegar and season with salt and pepper.
10. Mix together dill and mayo.
11. Build smørrebrød by laying out slices of rye bread and spreading dill mayonnaise on each slice.
12. Use a fork to flake meat off of the mackerel and layer on bread.
13. Top with apple slaw.
14. Enjoy with a bit of schnapps or Gammel Danske if you can get your hands on it. Skol!

Bacon and Smoked Mushroom Linguine

Makes 2 servings

Creamy alfredo-style sauce with smoked mushrooms, bacon, and asparagus over linguine.

Ingredients

- 4 oz dry linguine
- 6 button or crimini mushrooms
- 3 Tbsp vegetable oil
- 1 shallot, finely diced
- 2 cloves garlic, minced
- ¼ of a medium-sized onion, sliced
- ¼ cup white wine
- ½ cup cubed bacon
- 1 cup heavy cream
- 1 tsp Worcestershire sauce
- ¼ cup shredded parmesan cheese
- 6 asparagus spears
- Salt and pepper
- Fresh basil to garnish

Directions

1. Smoke mushrooms with Hickory Bisquettes for 1½ hours at 212–248°F (100–120°C).
2. Preheat grill for the asparagus.
3. Slice mushrooms and set aside.
4. Bring 1½ L of salted water to a boil, add linguine noodles, return to a boil, and cook for 8–10 minutes or until it is al dente, stirring frequently.
5. Drain pasta in a colander and run under cold water to stop the cooking process.
6. Toss pasta in 1 Tbsp of vegetable oil.
7. Heat 1 Tbsp of oil in a saucepan on medium heat.
8. Add shallots, garlic, and onions and cook until onions are translucent, approximately 3–5 minutes, then deglaze with white wine.
9. Add cubed bacon and cook until most of the fat has been rendered. Remove excess bacon fat from the pan with a spoon.
10. Add the smoked mushrooms and pour in heavy cream. Allow to reduce over low-medium heat for 10 minutes while stirring frequently.
11. Toss asparagus in 1 Tbsp of vegetable oil and season with salt and pepper. Grill on preheated grill for 3–5 minutes per side.
12. Stir Worcestershire sauce into thickened cream sauce.
13. Add pasta to the saucepan and coat pasta evenly in sauce.
14. Stir in parmesan cheese.
15. Season to taste with salt and pepper.
16. Serve pasta garnished with chopped basil leaves and grilled asparagus.

Soba Noodle Salad with Asian Smoked Duck

Makes 4 servings

Sesame and ginger marinated duck breast over cold soba noodle salad.

Ingredients
- 2 duck breasts

For Marinade
- ¼ cup vegetable oil
- 2 Tbsp sesame oil
- 1 Tbsp rice wine vinegar
- ¼ cup soy sauce
- 1 tsp grated ginger

For Soba Noodle Salad
- 250 g (½ lb or 6½ cups) soba or buckwheat noodles
- 1 Tbsp vegetable oil
- ½ cup shitake mushrooms, sliced
- ½ cup zucchini, sliced

- ¼ of a small red cabbage
- 3 cloves garlic
- ¼ cup white wine
- 1 red bell pepper, finely diced
- 1 medium-sized carrot, grated
- 2 green onions, thinly sliced
- ½ cup soy sauce
- 2 Tbsp balsamic
- 2 Tbsp tahini
- 1 tsp sesame oil
- 1–3 tsp sriracha sauce (depending on spice level preference)
- 1 Tbsp honey
- 3 Tbsp sesame seeds

Directions
1. Whisk together ingredients for the marinade.
2. Marinate duck breasts overnight.
3. Score the skin of the duck breasts, being careful not to pierce the skin and only cut the fat cap.
4. Smoke breasts for 1–2 hours with Oak Bisquettes at 212–239°F (100–115°C) or until an internal temperature of 158°F (70°C) is reached.
5. Remove from smoker and let cool.
6. Bring a saucepan filled with 6 cups water to a rolling boil.
7. Add soba noodles and simmer for 6–7 minutes, stirring occasionally.
8. Drain noodles and run under cold water, then transfer to a large bowl.
9. Heat vegetable oil in a large skillet.
10. Sauté mushrooms, zucchini, cabbage, and garlic in skillet. Deglaze with white wine and cool until vegetables are tender.
11. Add to bowl of soba noodles.
12. Mix in diced bell pepper, grated carrot, and sliced green onion.
13. Whisk together soy sauce, balsamic vinegar, tahini, sesame oil, sriracha sauce, and honey.
14. Dress soba noodle salad with dressing.
15. Slice cool duck and arrange over soba noodle salad.
16. Garnish with sesame seeds.

Chardonnay Marinated Salmon with Creamy Dill-Cucumber Sauce

Makes 2 servings

Lightly marinated salmon smoked and served with a creamy dill-cucumber sauce.

Ingredients
- 1 side of salmon

For Marinade
- ¾ cup Chardonnay
- ¼ cup canola oil
- ½ tsp salt
- 1 tsp dried dill
- 2 Tbsp fresh chopped dill
- 5–6 pink peppercorns

For Creamy Dill-Cucumber Sauce
- ½ long English cucumber
- 1 cup sour cream
- ½ bunch fresh dill, chopped

Directions
1. Whisk together ingredients for marinade.
2. Marinate deboned and scaled side of salmon overnight in the fridge.
3. Smoke salmon skin side down with Pacific Blend Bisquettes for two hours at 122°F (50°C).
4. Raise smoker temperature to 158°F (70°C) and smoke for another two hours.
5. Raise smoker temperature to 194°F (90°C) and smoke for a final hour.
6. Shred cucumber.
7. Mix together shredded cucumber with other sauce ingredients and serve with salmon once cooled.

Smoked Bison Burgers

Makes 4 servings

Whiskey Oak smoked bison with a spicy blueberry BBQ sauce and blue cheese.

Ingredients

- 4 buns of your choice
- 50 g (3 Tbsp) Danish blue cheese
- 2 Roma tomatoes, sliced
- 1 small head of butter lettuce
- ¼ cup mayonnaise
- ¼ cup blueberry BBQ Sauce

For Blueberry BBQ Sauce
- 2 cups blueberries
- ¾ cup ketchup
- ½ cup red wine vinegar
- ½ cup brown sugar
- 1 Tbsp molasses
- ½ cup water

- 2–4 tsp hot sauce (to taste)
- 1–3 tsp cayenne pepper (to taste)
- 1 tsp black pepper
- 2 cloves garlic, crushed

For Bison Burgers
- 600 g (1.3 lb) ground bison
- 4 Tbsp red onion, minced
- 2 cloves garlic, minced
- 2 Tbsp parsley, chopped
- 2 tsp salt
- ½ tsp black pepper
- 2 Tbsp blueberry BBQ Sauce

Directions
1. Combine all blueberry BBQ sauce ingredients in a saucepan and bring to a boil.
2. Simmer for 5–7 minutes.
3. Remove from heat and let cool.
4. Remove garlic cloves.
5. Blend sauce with a hand blender or in a regular blender until smooth.
6. Combine together all ingredients for burgers and form into four patties.
7. Smoke with Whiskey Oak Bisquettes for one hour at 225–250°F or until an internal temperature of 160°F (71°C) has been reached.
8. Build burgers on buns with mayonnaise, blueberry BBQ Sauce, Danish blue cheese, lettuce, and tomato.

Smoked Chocolate Bacon Truffles

Makes approximately 25 truffles

Smoked dark chocolate ganache stuffed with maple candied bacon and dipped in dark chocolate.

Ingredients

For Maple Candied Bacon
- 6 slices good quality smoked bacon
- 3 Tbsp maple syrup
- ¼ cup brown sugar
- ½ tsp salt

For Smoked Truffle Ganache
- 300 g (2⅓ cups) dark chocolate, roughly chopped

- 20 g (1½ Tbsp) butter
- 120 mL (½ cup) heavy cream
- 15 mL (1 Tbsp) whiskey

For Dipping
- 150 g (1 ¹⁄₁₀ cups) dark chocolate
- 1 Tbsp butter

Directions
1. Preheat oven to 350°F.
2. Combine maple syrup, brown sugar, and salt in a bowl.
3. Add bacon to the bowl and coat bacon with mixture.
4. Cover a rimmed baking sheet in aluminum foil and place a cooling rack over top.
5. Lay out coated bacon slices evenly spaced on the rack.
6. Add any remaining sugar mixture to the bacon so it is completely coated.
7. Bake for 40 minutes.
8. Once cooled, chop bacon into small cubes.
9. Smoke 300 g dark chocolate in an aluminum tray with Maple Bisquettes at 104°F (40°C) for 1 hour. Place an aluminum tray filled with ice underneath the chocolate to help regulate the temperature and reduce melting.
10. Melt chocolate and butter in a double boiler.
11. Once melted, stir in heavy cream until combined.
12. Remove from heat and whisk in whiskey.
13. Pour ganache into a heatproof container.
14. Let cool to room temperature, then place in fridge overnight.
15. Using an ice cream scoop or sturdy metal spoon, scrape out a ball of ganache.
16. Press a few pieces of maple candied bacon into the center of the ball of ganache.
17. Roll ganache between your palms until bacon is covered and chocolate is round, though there's no need for it to be perfectly round.
18. Place truffle on a baking tray lined with parchment paper.
19. Repeat with remaining truffle ganache.
20. Place tray in the fridge to cool truffles.

21. Melt 150g (1$\frac{1}{10}$ cups) dark chocolate in a double boiler, add 1 Tbsp butter once melted.
22. Remove from heat.
23. Dip truffles one at a time into melted chocolate, removing them with a fork.
24. Shake off any excess chocolate and return to tray.
25. Repeat with remaining truffles.
26. Return dipped truffles to the fridge and allow chocolate to harden.

Smoked Sea Salt Caramels

Makes 10–30 caramels depending on size and shape cut

Soft caramel candies sprinkled with smoked sea salt.

Ingredients
- 1 Tbsp coarse sea salt
- 250 mL (1 cup) heavy cream
- 4 Tbsp unsalted butter
- 2 tsp salt
- 300 g (1½ cup) granulated sugar
- ¼ cup maple syrup
- ¼ cup water
- 1 tsp vanilla

Directions
1. Place sea salt in an aluminum baking tray and smoke for 18–20 hours with Oak Bisquettes. Stir salt a couple of times while smoking. As this process takes some time, consider smoking more salt for future recipes where you want to add a bit of smoke without turning on the smoker.
2. Prepare an 8"x8" glass baking dish by lining with greased parchment paper.
3. Heat cream and butter in a small saucepan over medium heat until butter melts, remove from heat.
4. In a large pot, combine table salt, sugar, maple syrup, and water.
5. Use a wet pastry brush to wipe the sides of the pot to remove any crystallized sugar from the edges.
6. Position a candy thermometer so it is immersed in the sugar.
7. Boil sugar mixture over medium heat until a temperature of 315°F is reached, do not stir.
8. Remove from heat and whisk in cream-butter mixture.
9. Return pot to heat and bring the temperature back up to 250°F without stirring, remove from heat.
10. Whisk in vanilla.
11. Pour caramel into the prepared pan.
12. Sprinkle smoked sea salt overtop of caramels and let set uncovered overnight at room temperature.
13. Once set, remove caramels from baking dish by lifting parchment paper.
14. Turn over onto cutting board and cut into desired shapes.
15. Wrap caramels in wax paper and store at room temperature.

Smoked Peach Cobbler

Makes 4–6 servings

Sweet and smoky peach filling lightened with fresh basil and topped with flaky biscuit.

Ingredients
- 4 ripe peaches

For Filling
- 2 Tbsp granulated sugar
- 2 Tbsp brown sugar
- ¼ tsp cinnamon
- ¼ tsp nutmeg
- Juice and zest from ½ of a lemon
- 1 tsp cornstarch
- 5–6 leaves of basil, chopped

For Biscuit Topping
- ½ cup all-purpose flour
- 5 Tbsp granulated sugar
- 2 Tbsp brown sugar
- ½ tsp baking powder
- ¼ tsp salt
- 3 Tbsp butter
- 2 Tbsp water
- 1 tsp cinnamon

Directions
1. Peel, quarter, and pit peaches.
2. Arrange in small aluminum trays and smoke at 104°F (40°C) for one hour with Maple Bisquettes.
3. Remove from smoker and let cool.
4. Thinly slice peaches and set aside.
5. Preheat oven to 425°F.
6. Combine peaches with remaining filling ingredients.
7. Pour into ceramic baking dish.
8. Mix biscuit topping flour, 2 Tbsp granulated sugar, brown sugar, baking powder, and salt in a bowl.
9. Cut in butter to create a coarse crumble.
10. Add water and stir until combined.
11. Roll dough into small balls and drop over filling in ceramic dish.
12. Mix together cinnamon and remaining granulated sugar and sprinkle over cobbler.
13. Bake for 30 minutes or until biscuit topping is golden brown.
14. Serve warm with vanilla ice cream or whipped cream.

Jalapeño and Cheese Bear Bratwurst

Makes 8–12 servings

Bear meat is often regarded as being off-flavor and undesirable. Use this recipe and make bear jalapeño and cheese bear bratwurst, and you'll be the hit of your next party.

Ingredients
- 6 lbs lean bear meat
- ¼ lb high temperature cheddar cheese
- ½ cup diced jalapeños
- 5 oz Hi Mountain Original Bratwurst seasoning blend
- Casing
- ½ cup water

Directions
1. Trim all fat off the bear meat; you want nice lean meat with no fat.
2. Drain the juice and rinse your jalapeños very well, then dice into small pieces.
3. Portion out 5 oz of Hi Mountain Original Bratwurst seasoning blend.
4. Rinse casing well and flush the inside of the casing to remove all salt. Allow casing to soak in cool water to rehydrate for 1 hour before stuffing.
5. Sprinkle seasonings evenly over the meat and add ½ cup of water to mix and blend the seasonings. Mix well by hand.
6. Grind meat through standard sausage plate.
7. Now add cheese and jalapeños. Do not grind the cheese and jalapeños.
8. Use a filling horn grinder attachment or vertical stuffer to stuff into the clean casing.
9. Rope or link the product, and you are ready to smoke.
10. Place your brats in your Bradley Smoker and dry the surface of the casings at 150°F for 1 hour.
11. Increase the temperature to 160°F and turn on smoke generator for 2 hours using your personal favorite Bradley Smoker Bisquettes. I prefer Hickory for this product.
12. Increase temperature to 190°F until an internal temperature of 156°F is reached.

Elk Summer Sausage

Makes 10 servings

This is a great recipe for summer! Smoke 'em if you got 'em, and you'll have a great meal to serve. You didn't go that far to get elk just to fry it, right?

Ingredients
- 5 lbs lean elk meat
- 1 lb beef chuck roast
- ¼ cup nonfat dry milk
- 6 oz Hi Mountains Summer Sausage mix
- 3 sausage casings
- 1 cup cold water

Directions
1. Trim all fat off your elk meat. We will use a beef chuck roast to add some additional beef fat, which contains better flavor than elk fat.
2. Dice all meat into 1–2 inch cubes. Large cubes of meat will not blend as well with the seasonings as small cubes.
3. Portion 6 oz of Hi Mountains Summer Sausage mix. Hi Mountain has several blends; you may use any of their blends with this recipe.
4. Soak 3 fibrous summer sausage casings in cool water. This will allow them to rehydrate and increase the flexibility of the casing to reduce breakage when stuffing.
5. Evenly spread the seasonings and the nonfat dry milk across the meat and add 1 cup of cold water to the meat. Mix well to blend the seasonings with the meat. The nonfat dry milk will act as a binder and increase the meat's ability to retain water. This will aid in making a nice moist large diameter sausage product.
6. Grind all the meat twice through a ⅛-inch grinder plate. Remember, the finer you grind it, the tighter the meat will bind together, which is important on these large diameter products.
7. Stuff into the fibrous casings. You may find it helpful to make smaller length tubes so they fit on the racks of your Bradley Smoker.
8. Smoking large diameter products takes time. Remember low and slow. Preheat your smoke cabinet to 160°F and allow the product to smoke with your favorite Bradley Smoker Bisquettes for 3 hours. This will set the proteins in the meat so the fat will not melt out.
9. Turn the temperature up to 180°F for an additional 2 hours with the smoke generator turned off. At this time, the surface of the casing will be dry and the product will have absorbed all the smoke flavor possible.
10. Increase the cabinet temperature to 190°F for 1 hour or until an internal temperature of 156°F is reached.

Ground Moose Jerky

Makes 10 servings

A moose makes a lot of meat; along with a freezer full of steaks comes a second freezer full of ground meat! Ground jerky is a great way to help use several packages each month.

Ingredients
- 5 lbs ground moose meat (can be thawed out from the freezer or fresh)
- 1 pkg Hi Mountains Hunters Blend jerky seasoning (or your favorite blend)
- 1 pkg cure mix
- 1 cup cold water

Directions
1. Place all your ground meat in a mixing pan.
2. Add 1 pkg of Hi Mountain Hunters Blend seasoning mix and 1 pkg of cure mix.
3. Use 1 cup of cold water to mix the seasonings and add moisture for easy extruding.
4. To prepare a fine ground jerky that will be similar to whole muscle jerky, grind the meat 2 additional times with a ⅛-inch plate. For a coarse hamburger-type jerky, simply mix and use a jerky shooter gun to extrude nice strips of jerky onto the racks of your Bradley Smoker.
5. Dehydrator mesh helps to keep the product from sticking to the stainless smokehouse racks and also makes it easy to put on the racks and remove from the racks.
6. Place the racks into your Bradley Smoker. If you like a heavy strong smoke, begin smoking immediately. For a mild smoke flavor, dry the surface for 1 hour before turning on the Bradley Smoke generator.
7. Set temperature to 150°F for 1 hour. Continue to increase the temperature in your Bradley Smoker by 10°F each hour until the product is dried and ready to eat.
8. Drying jerky correctly can be a difficult process. The method I use may seem unconventional, but there is no simple solution. I remove my strips one by one and squeeze the strip hard to see if I can feel moisture inside the strip. If you bend the strip and it breaks, it's overdried. Find the middle between drying all the moisture of the strip and making it still flexible, and you will have it. Now write the process down and repeat.

Hickory Smoked Turkey Bacon

Makes 10 servings

How do you get bacon from a turkey? Well, that's the fun part—and it's a lot healthier than pork bacon!

Ingredients
- 5 lbs boneless turkey drums and thighs
- 3 Tbsp Bradley Honey cure
- 1 Tbsp dark brown sugar
- 1 cup nonfat dry milk
- ½ cup cold water

Directions
1. Place boneless turkey meat into pan and add seasonings. Just cover to the top of the meat with cold water. Place in refrigerator for 48 hours to brine.
2. After 48 hours, drain any leftover brine and rinse well with cold water.
3. Grind half the meat through a ⅛-inch grinder plate and half through a coarse sausage plate.
4. Add 1 cup of nonfat dry milk as a binder along with ½ cup water to assist mixing. Mix 2–5 minutes or until the meat becomes a paste.
5. Spray a shallow aluminum pan with nonstick spray and fill the pan to a depth of 3 inches. Use as many pans as needed.
6. Preheat the smoker to 160°F and load the pans onto the racks of your Bradley Smoker.
7. Dry the surface of the product for 1 hour, then turn on the smoke generator and apply smoke for 1 hour. This product will be very wet and absorb smoke quickly, so be careful not to oversmoke.
8. Increase cabinet temperature to 180°F for 1 hour, then increase to 200°F until an internal temperature of 145°F is achieved.
9. Slice and fry in the same manner as pork bacon.

Mesquite Smoked Cracked Pepper and Garlic Venison Snack Sticks

Makes 10 servings

This household favorite is a fun snack that's easy to make.

Ingredients

- 5 lbs lean venison trimmings
- 4 oz Hi Mountain Seasonings Cracked Pepper and Garlic Snack Stick mix (or your favorite recipe)
- 1 cup of cold water
- Casing

Directions

1. Place your venison trimmings into a mixing pan and add 4 oz of seasoning blend.
2. Add ½ cup water to mix and blend the seasonings, then grind through a ⅛-inch plate.
3. Add ¼ cup of water to the ground product, mix lightly, and grind a second time through the same grinder plate.
4. It's important that this product be very wet in order to stuff correctly and rehydrate the mahogany collagen casings. This will also keep the product moist during the smoking process.
5. Add an additional ¼ cup of water, mix lightly again, and stuff into the casings.
6. This product is small in diameter, so the surface will dry quickly. Presmoke the Bradley Smoker cabinet without applying heat. Only turn on the smoke generator and cold smoke for 1 hour.
7. After 1 hour turn the cabinet temperature to 140°F and continue to smoke for an additional hour.
8. Increase the cabinet temperature in your Bradley Smoker to 180°F and turn off the smoke generator. Remain at 180°F for 1 hour.
9. Increase the cabinet temperature to 190°F and finish the product to an internal temperature of 158°F.

Polish Venison Smoked Sausage

Makes 10 servings

Breakfast is the best meal of the day, so start out right with some healthy and lean venison smoked sausage.

Ingredients
- 5 lbs lean venison trimmings
- 1 lb smoked bacon
- 6 oz Hi Mountain Seasonings Polish seasoning
- Casing
- 1 cup water

Directions
1. Trim all the fat out of your venison trimmings. Venison fat has a caulk texture, which is undesirable in sausage products, so be sure to trim all the fat possible. Cut trimmings into 1–2 inch cubes.
2. Dice 1 lb of smoked bacon into small pieces approximately ½ the size of your venison cubes. This will allow the grinder to blend the fat well with the lean venison when grinding. This smoked bacon will give you a smooth smoked flavor all the way through the center of your sausage product.
3. Portion 6 oz of Hi Mountains Polish seasoning. You may add additional pepper, salt, or brown sugar to change the flavor profile if you so desire.
4. Rinse your hog casings inside and outside to remove all the preservative salt. Allow the clean casings to remain in cool water for at least 1 hour to rehydrate before stuffing. This will reduce casing breakage.
5. Spread seasonings evenly across the meat, add 1 cup of water to mix and blend the seasonings. Mix well until seasonings begin to absorb into the meat. Always remember that moisture allows the seasoning to penetrate into the meat. Seasonings do not penetrate well on dry surfaces. This additional moisture will also help prevent the product from drying out in your Bradley Smoker.
6. Grind 3 lbs of the meat through a fine ⅛-inch grinder plate.
7. Grind 3 lbs of the meat through a coarse sausage plate.
8. Mix the two 3 lbs batches of ground sausage together and blend well by hand. This will give the product a desirable texture, bite, and mouth feel.
9. Stuff into your rinsed hog casings and rope or link the sausage product.
10. For a strong smoked sausage, presmoke the cabinet for 15 minutes before placing the product inside your Bradley Smoker. This will allow the casings to begin absorbing that good Bradley Smoker flavor immediately.
11. Place your sausage in the cabinet and set the temperature at 160°F for 2 hours.
12. Increase the smokehouse temperature to 180°F for 2 hours and turn off the smoker generator.
13. Finish the product to a final internal temperature of 156°F.

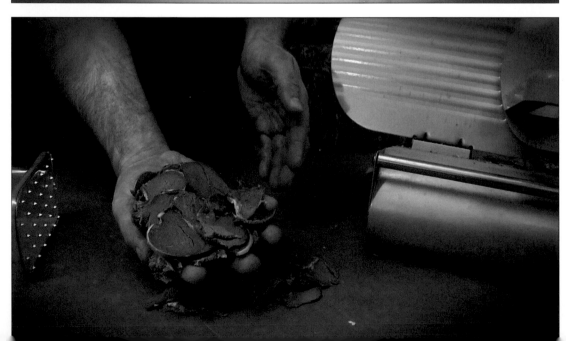

Smoked Venison Ham

Makes 8–10 servings

After your taste your first smoked venison ham, you may want to change your Easter dinner plans!

Ingredients
- 1 bone-in venison hind quarter
- 5 Tbsp Bradley Sugar Ham cure
- 1 Tbsp dark brown sugar
- 1 Tbsp white salt
- 8 cups cold water

Directions
1. Mix the dry seasonings with 8 cups cold water and stir until completely dissolved.
2. Using a multihole injection needle, inject brine in a grid pattern and place injection spots one inch apart. Inject both sides of the hind quarter.
3. Cover ham and place in refrigerator for 4 days to allow brine to soak into the muscles.
4. After 4 days, remove the ham and rinse well with cold water.
5. Preheat Bradley Smoker to 170°F. This is a large product with a lot of surface area, so it will take quite some time to dry the surface.
6. Dry for 2 hours at 170°F, then turn on the smoke generator and increase the temperature to 180° F for 2 hours.
7. Increase the cabinet temperature to 200°F until an internal temperature of 156°F is reached.

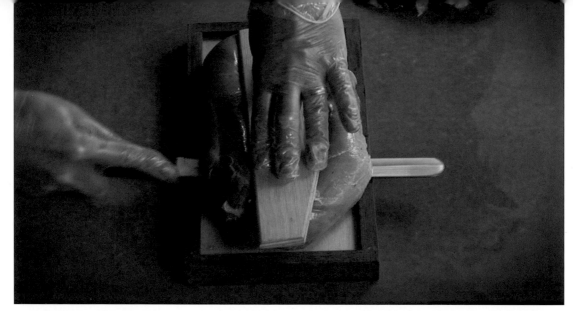

Whole Muscle Turkey Jerky

Makes 8–10 servings

Everyone loves jerky, and turkey jerky is the best. The muscle holds moisture well and absorbs flavor and seasoning better than venison.

Ingredients
- 5 lbs sliced turkey breast
- 3 tsp seasoned salt
- 2 tsp fine black pepper
- 1 tsp onion salt
- 1 tsp garlic salt
- 2 tsp white salt
- ½ tsp cure salt preservative
- ¼ cup water

Directions
1. Debone your wild turkey breast and slice the strips ¼-inch thick.
2. Add the above seasonings or your favorite seasoning blend.
3. Mix in ¼ cup of water to mix the seasonings with the sliced turkey breast.
4. Cover or vacuum seal and allow meat to rest for 24 hours before smoking.
5. This product will absorb smoke quickly, so allow the surface of the meat to dry in the Bradley Smoker for 1½ hours at 150°F.
6. Turn the smoke generator on for 40 minutes to apply a light smoke flavor using Maple or Alder Bisquettes. Hickory and Mesquite may create too strong a smoke flavor.
7. Increase smokehouse temperature to 170°F for 1 hour.
8. Dry product to feel. When squeezing the product, if you feel moisture in the center of the strip dry longer. Do not overdry. Be sure the strips will still bend and flex. If they break, then you are overdrying your jerky. Dry the strips to be firm but flexible at 180°F. Remember, low and slow.

Wild Boar Hot Sausage

Makes 6–10 servings

Wild boar can be strong in flavor, so I'm going to share with you a great recipe with strong ingredients to make your family fall in love with wild boar meat.

Ingredients
- 4½ lbs lean wild boar trimmings
- ½ lb domestic pork back fat
- 4 oz Hi Mountains Italian Sausage seasoning
- 1 tsp of crushed red pepper
- ½ tsp of cayenne pepper
- 1 cup cold water
- Casing

Directions:
1. Clean casings. This is very important. Rinse them well inside and out and allow to soak in cool water to rehydrate. This will help prevent broken casings.
2. Dice the pork back fat into small pieces so it blends well with the lean boar meat when grinding.
3. Add all dry seasonings.
4. Use the cold water to mix and blend the seasonings.
5. Grind half the meat block through a ⅛-inch plate and the other half through a coarse sausage plate.
6. Mix well and stuff into 32–35 mm hog casings.
7. Serve with your favorite marinara sauce and fried peppers and onions.

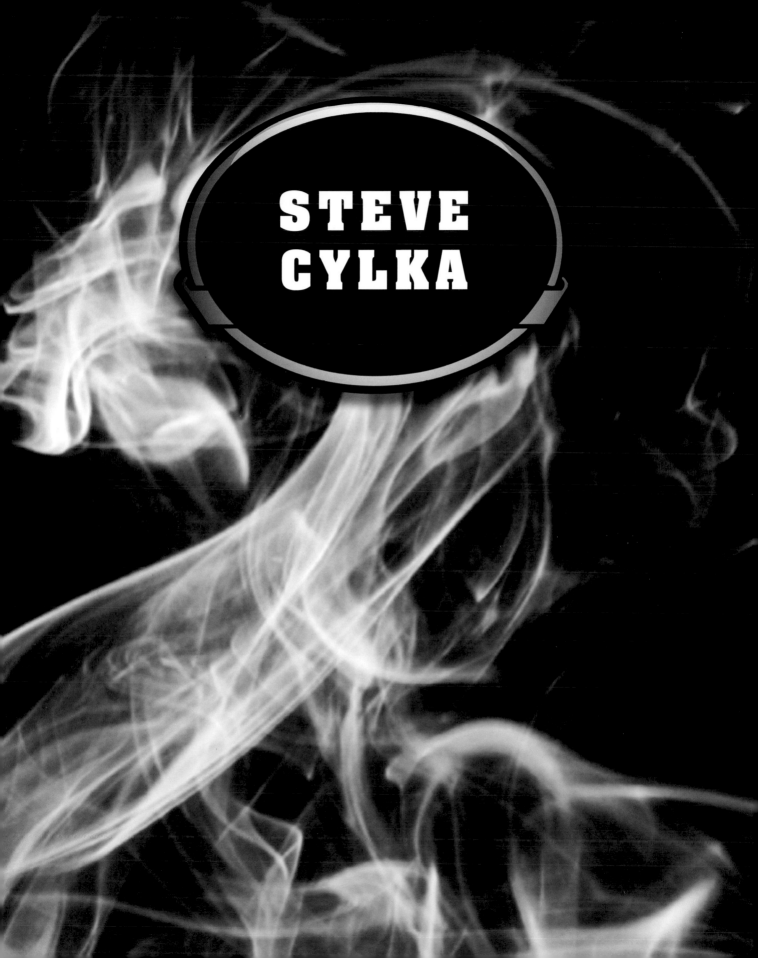

Cajun Smoked Catfish

Makes 4 servings

This recipe uses the spicy blend of blackened seasoning that made catfish a popular Cajun dish. Smoked catfish is light, delicate, and complemented nicely by the Cajun spices.

Ingredients
- 4 catfish fillets
- ¾ cup oil
- 1 tsp paprika
- 1 tsp garlic powder
- ½ tsp onion powder
- ½ tsp thyme
- ½ tsp oregano
- ½ tsp ground black pepper
- ¼ tsp cayenne pepper
- 1½ tsp salt

Directions
1. Mix all ingredients except catfish togther to make a marinade. Place catfish in a shallow baking dish or bowl. Pour marinade on the fish and turn them to ensure they are evenly coated.
2. Cover the dish with plastic wrap and place in the fridge for 1 hour.
3. Start smoker with Pacific Blend Bisquettes and set it for 225°F.
4. Place catfish on racks and put in the smoker.
5. Smoke the fish for 2⅓ hours.

Cherrywood Smoked Double Garlic Kielbasa

Makes about 4 rings of kielbasa

Make kielbasa right at home that is better than anything you could buy at your local European deli. The spice blend with extra garlic gives the kielbasa a deep flavor profile and the cherrywood provides light smoky notes.

Ingredients
- 5 lbs pork shoulder or fresh ham
- 2½ Tbsp garlic powder
- 3 tsp coarse kosher salt
- 3 tsp ground black pepper
- 2 tsp dried oregano
- 1 cup cold water
- ½ cup skim milk powder
- 1 tsp cure #1
- Casings

Directions
1. Run the pork through a meat grinder using the coarse mincing plate. Place meat in a large mixing bowl.
2. In another bowl, mix together the garlic powder, salt, black pepper, oregano, water, milk powder, and cure until somewhat dissolved. Pour over the meat. Knead together so everything is thoroughly combined and all the meat has been coated in the spice mixture. Place in the fridge and let the meat mixture marinate for about 3 hours.
3. Take the meat mixture out of the fridge and stuff the sausage casings with the meat according to the instructions of the sausage stuffer. Make sure to tie the ends of the casings well.
4. Preheat the smoker for 130°F with Cherrywood Bisquettes.
5. Place the kielbasa in the smoker either by laying them on the smoker racks or hanging them using Bradley Smoker Hooks. Make sure the kielbasa are not touching one another.
6. Each hour, increase the temperature of the smoker by 20°F. So, the first hour is set at 130°F, the second hour at 150°F, the third hour at 170°F, and the fourth hour at 190°F. Leave the smoker at 190°F for the remainder of the smoke.
7. Once the internal temperature of the kielbasa has reached 165°F, remove them from the smoker. The smoking time takes around 4 hours, although it can take longer if there is a lot of meat in the smoker.
8. Hang the kielbasa for 1–2 hours before storing. The best way to store kielbasa is to vacuum seal them in food-safe bags and place in the freezer for up to 3 months.

Maple Smoked Bacon

Makes 5 pounds of bacon

Almost everything is better when homemade, but it has never been more true than with homemade bacon. This bacon is marinated with maple syrup during the curing process and then smoked with maple wood.

Ingredients
- 5 lbs pork belly
- 3 Tbsp coarse kosher salt
- 3 Tbsp brown sugar
- 1 tsp cure #1
- ⅓ cup maple syrup

Directions
1. Trim the pork belly by removing any loose pieces of fat.
2. In a large bowl, mix together the salt, brown sugar, cure, and maple syrup.
3. Place pork belly in a large freezer bag or food-safe vacuum seal bag. Pour the mixture into the bag and seal it. Rotate the bag, ensuring that the pork belly is completely coated. Cover with plastic wrap and place in the fridge.
4. Leave the pork belly in the fridge for 4 days, flipping it twice a day.
5. After curing for 4 days, rinse the pork belly thoroughly under cold water.
6. Place the pork belly in the fridge for 8 hours. This dries the outside of the meat, enhancing the smoking process.
7. Set the smoker to 200°F using Maple Bisquettes.
8. Use Bradley Sausage Hooks to hang the pork belly in the smoker.
9. Smoke the pork belly until it reaches an internal temperature of 155°F. This can take about 4 hours.
10. Remove the bacon from the smoker and let it rest for 1 hour.
11. Use a knife to remove the skin or rind from the bacon.
12. If desired, brush some more maple syrup on the bacon.
13. Once cooled, the bacon can be sliced using a meat slicer.

Competition Smoked BBQ Ribs

Makes 4 servings

Smoking ribs is usually one of the first projects for any new Bradley Smoker, and it has never been easier than with this recipe. These ribs are sweet, sticky, smokey, and worthy of any ribfest event.

Ingredients
- 2 racks pork back ribs
- ⅔ cup packed brown sugar
- 3 Tbsp paprika
- 2 Tbsp white sugar
- 1½ Tbsp salt
- 1 Tbsp ground black pepper
- 1½ tsp dry mustard
- 1 tsp cayenne pepper
- 1 tsp thyme
- 1 tsp ground cumin
- ½ tsp ground sage
- ½ cup beer
- 1½ cup BBQ sauce

Directions
1. Peel the membrane off the back of each rack of ribs. Generously rub the brown sugar all over the ribs. Place in the fridge for 2–3 hours.
2. Set smoker to 225°F using wood Bisquettes of choice (Hickory, Pecan, and Whiskey Oak work great for ribs).
3. Make the rub by mixing together the paprika, white sugar, salt, black pepper, mustard, cayenne, thyme, cumin, and sage together. Rub the spice mixture all over the ribs. Place the ribs in the smoker and smoke for 3 hours.
4. Remove the ribs from the smoker and wrap each rack in heavy duty aluminum foil. Pour ¼ cup beer with each rack of ribs before folding up the foil. Place the wrapped ribs back in the smoker and cook for another hour.
5. Remove the ribs from the smoker and take out of the aluminum foil. Generously coat the ribs with BBQ sauce. Place the ribs back in the smoker and smoker for one final hour.
6. Let them rest for 10 minutes before cutting and serving.

Smoked Buffalo Chicken Wings

Makes 4 servings

Take buffalo wings to the next level by smoking them! These wings have all the classic flavors of hot sauce and blue cheese with the additional smoky notes. Perfect for tailgating!

Ingredients
- 2 lbs chicken wings
- 1½ cups hot sauce, divided
- 1 tsp salt
- 1 tsp cayenne pepper
- 3 Tbsp butter
- 2 tsp sugar
- 1 tsp garlic powder
- ½ cup crumbled blue cheese
- ¾ cup diced celery

Directions
1. Cut each chicken wing into three portions: drumette, middle portion, and tips. Discard the tips of the wings and place the other portions in a large bowl.
2. Mix together ½ cup hot sauce with salt and cayenne pepper. Pour over the wings and toss so all the wings are coated in the hot sauce marinade.
3. Place in the fridge and let the wings marinate for 1–2 hours.
4. Set up the smoker for 250°F using wood Bisquettes of choice.
5. Lay wings on smoker racks and smoke for 2–2½ hours.
6. While the wings are smoking, make the buffalo sauce. In a saucepan, melt the butter on medium heat. Whisk in the remaining hot sauce, sugar, and garlic powder. Simmer for 5–10 minutes. Remove from heat.
7. Remove wings from the smoker and toss with the buffalo sauce.
8. Top with crumbled blue cheese and celery.

Bacon Wrapped Chicken Breast Stuffed with Spinach and Cheese

Makes 4 servings

This recipe is pure smoked decadence. Tender smoked chicken breast, gooey cheesy spinach stuffing, and wrapped in bacon!

Ingredients

- 4 boneless skinless chicken breasts
- 8 bacon slices
- 1 Tbsp butter
- ½ onion, minced
- ½ tsp garlic powder
- 1 tsp paprika
- ½ tsp salt
- 3 cups fresh spinach
- 1 cup cream cheese, softened
- 1 cup grated cheddar cheese

Directions

1. Holding knife horizontally, insert into the thick end of each chicken breast and cut to make a deep pocket. Be careful not to pierce through the other end.
2. In a skillet, melt butter on medium heat. Add onion, garlic powder, paprika, and salt and cook until tender.
3. Add the spinach and stir until cooked and wilted. Remove from heat.
4. Stir the cream cheese and grated cheddar in with the cooked spinach.
5. Spoon the cheese and spinach mixture evenly into the pockets of each chicken breast.
6. Wrap each stuffed chicken breast with 2 slices of bacon. Place on smoker rack.
7. Set the smoker to 250°F using wood Bisquettes of choice (Oak, Maple, or Hickory work great).
8. Smoke the chicken breasts until they reach an internal temperature of 165°F.

Smoked Chipotle Maple Chicken Salad

Makes 4 servings

Bring the BBQ to a salad through these sweet and smoky chicken breasts. The sweet and spicy smoked chicken goes well with mixed greens and chopped veggies.

Ingredients
- 3 boneless skinless chicken breasts
- 1 tsp chipotle powder
- ½ tsp salt
- ½ tsp garlic powder
- ½ tsp onion powder
- ½ tsp ground black pepper
- ¼ cup maple syrup
- 4 cups mixed greens
- ½ english cucumber, cut into small chunks
- 12–16 grape tomatoes, halved
- 1½ cup Havarti cheese, cubed
- ⅔ cup ranch salad dressing (chipotle ranch, if available)

Directions
1. In a small bowl, mix together the chipotle powder, salt, garlic powder, onion powder, and black pepper.
2. Rub the spice mixture all over the chicken breasts and place them on the smoker rack.
3. Set the smoker to 250°F using wood Bisquettes of choice (Hickory, Apple, and Maple work great).
4. Smoke the chicken breasts until they reach an internal temperature of 165°F, which can take about 2½–3 hours.
5. During the smoking process, brush the chicken breasts with maple syrup after every hour. Brush them one final time once they are finished smoking.
6. Let the chicken breasts rest 10 minutes. Cut them into ¾-inch slices.
7. Assemble the salad on individual plates by laying some greens, chopped cucumber, grape tomatoes, and Havarti cheese. Top with some smoked chicken slices and drizzle with ranch dressing.
8. Serve immediately.

Smoked Meatloaf with Bacon Weave Wrap

Makes 4 servings

This recipe kicks meatloaf to the next level! Classic meatloaf wrapped in a weave of bacon and smoked to perfection.

Ingredients
- 2 lbs lean ground beef
- 1 onion, minced
- 1 red pepper, minced
- 3 garlic cloves, minced
- 1 egg, slightly beaten
- ½ cup bread crumbs
- 1½ tsp salt
- 1 Tbsp brown sugar
- 2 tsp paprika
- 1 tsp ground black pepper
- ½ tsp cayenne pepper
- ½ tsp oregano
- 16 bacon strips
- ⅔ cup BBQ sauce, divided

Directions
1. In a large bowl combine all ingredients except the bacon and ⅓ cup BBQ sauce.
2. Use your hands to knead the meat mixture until everything is fully combined and thoroughly mixed.
3. Mold the meat mixture into a log shape.
4. To make the bacon weave, lay eight bacon strips side by side vertically. Horizontally, weave the top bacon strip through the vertical strips. For the remaining horizontal strips, pull back every other vertical bacon strip. Lay a bacon strip down right next to the other horizontal strips. Pull the vertical strips back down. Do the same again but with the other vertical bacon strips. Do this for the remaining bacon until you have completed the bacon weave.
5. Place the meatloaf in the center of the bacon weave. Wrap the weave around the meatloaf and place the wrapped meatloaf fold side down on a smoker rack.
6. Start up the smoker using wood Bisquettes of choice (Hickory works well). Bring the smoker up to a temperature of 250°F.
7. Place the meatloaf in the smoker and cook until the internal temperature reaches 160°F.
8. Brush the remaining ⅓ cup BBQ sauce after the first 2 hours of smoking.

Smoked Salmon Nuggets with Maple Cream Dip

Makes 4–6 servings

Salmon is classic to smoke in the Bradley Smoker, and these nuggets turn this smoked fish into a great bite-sized appetizer. The creamy maple dip perfectly complements the salmon.

Ingredients
- 2 lbs fresh salmon fillets
- 1½ cups brown sugar
- ¾ cup coarse kosher salt
- 1 Tbsp garlic powder
- 1 Tbsp onion powder
- ½ Tbsp black pepper
- ½ tsp cayenne pepper
- 1 cup cream cheese
- ½ cup mayonnaise
- 1 Tbsp milk
- 3 Tbsp pure maple syrup

Directions
1. Wash the salmon under cold water. Carefully slice the skin off the salmon. Cut the salmon into 1-inch cubes.
2. Make the dry brine by mixing together the brown sugar, salt, garlic powder, onion powder, black pepper, and cayenne. Toss the salmon cubes in the dry brine, making sure that all sides of the salmon cubes are coated in the brine. Cover and place the salmon in the fridge for 6–8 hours.
3. Remove the salmon from the fridge and rinse under cold water to remove all the brine. Make sure that the salmon is thoroughly rinsed, otherwise the salmon could end up too salty.
4. Lay the salmon cubes on the Bradley Smoker racks, ensuring that they are not touching each other. Let the salmon cubes dry for about 60–90 minutes so they form a nice pellicle surface on them. Use a fan, if possible, to circulate the air.
5. Set the smoker to 130°F using Pacific Blend Bisquettes.
6. Place the salmon in the smoker. Smoke for about 3½ hours. After each hour, increase the temperature by 20°F (i.e.: 130°F for 1 hour, 150°F for 1 hour, 170°F for 1 hour, and 190°F for 30 minutes).
7. While the salmon is smoking, make the maple dip by mixing together the cream cheese, mayonnaise, milk, and maple syrup until smooth and creamy. If a thinner consistency is desired, mix in a little more milk. Place in the fridge until serving.
8. Serve the salmon warm or cold alongside the maple cream dip.

Smoked Shrimp Risotto

Makes 2 servings

Arborio rice in a creamy white wine sauce with mushrooms, parmesan cheese, and topped with smoked shrimp.

Ingredients

- 1 lb fresh shrimp, peeled and deveined
- 2 Tbsp oil
- 1 Tbsp dried oregano
- 1 tsp garlic powder
- 1 tsp salt
- 2 Tbsp butter
- 1 garlic clove, minced
- 1 onion, diced
- 3 cups mushrooms, thinly sliced
- 1½ cups arborio rice
- 1 cup white wine
- 3 cups chicken broth
- ½ cup parmesan cheese

Directions

1. In a large bowl, toss the shrimp with oil, oregano, garlic powder, and salt. Place the shrimp on smoker racks.
2. Set the smoker to 225°F using wood Bisquettes of choice (Alder, Apple, and Pacific Blend work great).
3. Smoke the shrimp until they turn pink. This can take 30–45 minutes.
4. Make the risotto by melting the butter in a saucepan on medium heat.
5. Add the onion, mushrooms, and garlic. Stir often until the onions are tender.
6. Add the arborio rice and cook for a few minutes, stirring constantly.
7. Pour in the wine and cook for 2–3 more minutes.
8. Add broth to the rice, ½ cup at a time, until the rice is cooked. Stir constantly.
9. Stir in the parmesan cheese.
10. If a creamier texture is desired, stir in a little more broth.
11. Spoon the risotto on a plate and top with smoked shrimp.

Steve's Smoked Tomato Soup

Makes 4–6 servings

This homemade soup recipe is smooth, creamy, and made with fresh smoked vegetables.

Ingredients
- 5–6 large tomatoes
- 2 red peppers
- 1 onion
- 4 Tbsp olive oil
- 2 tsp salt
- 1 tsp ground black pepper
- 3 cups vegetable or chicken broth
- ½ tsp cayenne pepper
- 1 cup 10% cream
- Salt and pepper to taste

Directions
1. Halve the tomatoes. Core and halve the peppers. Peel and cut the onion into ½-inch slices.
2. Lay the vegetables on the smoker racks cut side facing up. Drizzle the oil on the vegetables. Sprinkle the salt and pepper on the vegetables.
3. Set the smoker to 250°F using wood Bisquettes of choice.
4. Smoke the vegetables for 2½–3 hours so they are tender.
5. Using a blender or food processor, blend the smoked vegetables until smooth. If necessary add some of the broth to the blender to aid in the pureeing.
6. Pour the smoked vegetable puree into a soup pot and add the broth and cayenne pepper.
7. Bring the soup to a boil and then lower heat to a simmer.
8. Stir in the cream, salt and pepper to taste, and cook for 10 more minutes.
9. Serve soup hot.

Pasta with Smoked Pork Tenderloin and Tomato Basil Cream Sauce

Makes 4 servings

BBQ goes Italian with this delicious pasta dish. The pork tenderloin is moist with a light smoky flavor, served on a bed of pasta tossed in a creamy rose sauce with fresh torn basil.

Ingredients

- 1 pork tenderloin
- 1 tsp paprika
- 1 tsp salt
- 1 tsp garlic powder
- 1 tsp sugar
- 1 tsp dry basil
- 2 Tbsp oil
- 3 shallots, minced

- 1 garlic clove, minced
- 1 can (796 mL) diced tomatoes
- 1 Tbsp sugar
- ½ tsp salt
- 1 cup cream
- ½ cup parmesan cheese
- ¼ cup fresh basil, torn
- 440 g (1 lb) dry pasta (bowtie, penne, etc.)

Directions

1. Prepare the dry rub for the tenderloin by mixing together the paprika, 1 tsp salt, garlic powder, 1 tsp sugar, and dry basil. Rub all over the meat.
2. Set the smoker to 250°F using wood Bisquettes of choice (Whiskey Oak, Pecan, or Hickory work great).
3. Smoke the pork tenderloin until it reaches an internal temperature of 145°F. Let rest for 10 minutes before slicing.
4. In a saucepan, heat the oil on medium heat. Add the shallots and garlic. Cook, stirring often for a few minutes.
5. Stir in the can of diced tomatoes, 1 Tbsp sugar, and ½ tsp salt. Bring to a boil and then lower heat to a simmer.
6. Let the sauce simmer for 10 minutes.
7. Stir in the cream and parmesan cheese. Simmer for another 3–5 minutes. Remove from heat and stir in the fresh basil.
8. Cook pasta according to package directions. Strain.
9. Stir the sauce with the pasta.
10. Serve pasta with sliced smoked pork tenderloin.

Smoked Cheese

Makes 1–4 pounds of cheese

Cheese is one of the simplest things to smoke, and it is great on burgers, pasta, and more! This method works for almost any kind of cheese, including cheddar, mozzarella, Gouda, and many others.

Ingredients
- 1–4 lbs cheese blocks (cheddar, Gouda, mozzarella, provolone, Swiss, etc.)

Directions
1. Cut the cheese so that the pieces are not larger than 4" x 4" x 2"
2. If you desire, hook up the cold smoke adaptor to the Bradley Smoker.
3. Set the smoker so that the temperature does not go above 90°F. Wood Bisquettes that works well for smoking cheese include Apple, Cherry, Pecan, and Maple.
4. Place cheese on smoker racks 1 inch apart.
5. Smoke from 2–4 hours depending on desired level of smoke flavor.
6. Wrap smoked cheese individually in plastic wrap and place in the fridge for a minimum of 2 weeks before consuming. This resting period mellows the smoke flavor and allows the smoke to permeate the cheese.

Smoked Maple Beans

Makes 2–3 servings

Smoked maple beans might just be the ultimate side dish prepared in the Bradley Smoker. Great alongside pulled pork, ribs, burgers, and more!

Ingredients
- ½ lb bacon, diced
- 2 onions, diced
- 1 pepper, diced
- 3 cans navy beans, drained
- ⅓ cup maple syrup
- 1 cup brown sugar
- 2 cups ketchup
- 2 Tbsp Worcestershire sauce
- 1 tsp salt
- 1 tsp garlic powder
- 1½ tsp chili powder
- ½ tsp ground black pepper

Directions
1. In a frying pan, cook the bacon, onions, and pepper for about 10 minutes so the bacon is starting to brown and the vegetables are tender and translucent. Drain a bit of the bacon grease.
2. Mix with the remaining ingredients in a disposable aluminum pan.
3. Set the smoker to 225°F using wood Bisquettes of choice (Apple, Maple, or Jim Beam work great).
4. Smoke the beans for 3 hours, stirring every 45 minutes.

Smoked Pulled Pork

Makes 6–8 servings

Smoked pulled pork is true BBQ! Low and slow, the pork roast is rubbed down with a sweet spice blend and smoked until the meat just falls apart. Serve it on a bun or on its own with BBQ sauce.

Ingredients
- 1 pork roast (butt, shoulder, or blade)
- ¼ cup paprika
- ¼ cup sugar
- 3 Tbsp salt
- 2 Tbsp ground black pepper
- 1 Tbsp dry mustard
- 2 tsp dry oregano
- 2 tsp thyme
- 2 tsp cayenne pepper
- 2 tsp ground cumin

Directions
1. Make the rub by mixing together the sugar and all the spices. Generously rub the spice mixture all over the pork roast.
2. Set the smoker to 225°F using wood Bisquettes of choice (Apple, Cherry, Oak, or Jim Beam work great).
3. Smoke the pork roast until it reaches an internal temperature of 195°F. This can take 14–18 hours, depending on the outside temperature.
4. Pull the pork into thin strips.
5. Serve on a kaiser roll with BBQ sauce.

Dragon Jalapeño Poppers

Makes 16 poppers

These little bite-sized treats are fiery hot and full of smoking goodness. If you're making them for a party, be sure to prepare lots, since they will be gone in a flash.

Ingredients
- 8 jalapeño peppers
- ½ cup cream cheese
- ½ cup grated cheddar cheese
- 1 tsp chili powder
- 16 cocktail smokies
- 8 slices of bacon, cut in half

Directions
1. Slice the jalapeño peppers lengthwise. Using a knife, remove the seeds and membrane.
2. Mix together the cream cheese, cheddar cheese, and chili powder.
3. Fill the hollowed out portion of the jalapeño pepper with the cheese mixture.
4. Place a cocktail smokie on top of the cheese mixture.
5. Wrap half a slice of bacon around the jalapeño pepper. Use a toothpick if the bacon is falling off.
6. Set the smoker to 250°F using wood Bisquettes of choice (Pecan, Maple, or Hickory work great).
7. Smoke the poppers for 2–3 hours or until the bacon is browned.

KATHLEEN
DONEGAN

Applewood Smoked Fusion Turkey Breast with Cilantro-Lime Mayonnaise

Makes 2 servings

A delicious, juicy turkey will impress any guest, and the fresh mayonnaise elevates the taste buds and makes it the perfect meal.

Ingredients
- 3½ lb boneless turkey breast

For Marinade
- ½ cup dry white wine
- ¼ cup soy sauce
- ¼ cup sesame oil
- 3 Tbsp fresh lemon juice
- 1 Tbsp fresh thyme (or 1 tsp dry)

For Cilantro-Lime Mayonnaise
- 1¼ cup mayonnaise (homemade or the best you can get, no "salad dressing")
- Zest of 1 lime
- 2 Tbsp fresh lime juice
- 2 tsp jalapeño, seeded and minced
- 1½ tsp soy sauce
- 1 clove garlic, minced
- 1 tsp Dijon mustard
- 1 chopped cilantro or a mix*

Directions
1. Combine all marinade ingredients in a bowl or large food storage bag. Place turkey breast in marinade, turn to coat, and refrigerate. Marinate overnight or up to 24 hours, turning the turkey breast over several times to marinate evenly.
2. Heat smoker to 220°F using Apple Bisquettes.
3. Smoke the turkey approximately 2½ hours to an internal temperature of 165°F.
4. Mix all ingredients for cilantro-lime mayonnaise together and chill for at least one hour to allow flavors to combine.
5. Serve warm or at room temperature with cilantro-lime mayonnaise. The turkey can be sliced for sandwiches or as a main course, or cubed at room temperature as part of a buffet. It is very versatile.

*Tip: If you don't eat cilantro, flat leaf parsley can be substituted—but at some loss of flavor.

One-Pound Pork Tenderloin with Asian Rub and Cucumber Salad

Makes 2 servings

This is a recipe for pork tenderloin with a tangy Asian twist to it. The cucumber salad goes great with the pork tenderloin since the freshness of the salad complements the pork.

Ingredients for Tenderloin
- 1 lb pork tenderloin
- 1 Tbsp five spice powder
- 1 Tbsp ground ginger
- 1 Tbsp light brown sugar (or "Sugar in the Raw", demerara sugar)
- 1 Tbsp cracked Szechuan peppercorns (or more if you want more kick)
- 1 Tbsp granulated garlic
- ½ Tbsp salt
- About ¼ cup bacon fat (this holds the rub together and imparts even more flavor)

Directions
1. Mix the spices and bacon fat together well and smear the mixture all over the tenderloin. Refrigerate for at least 4 hours or overnight.
2. Let the tenderloin sit outside of the refrigerator for at least 1 hour before putting it in the smoker.
3. Heat the Bradley Smoker to 220°F.
4. Oil a rack well.
5. For the 1-lb tenderloin, the smoking time to an internal temperature of 160°F is about 2 hours.
6. Let it sit for a few minutes before slicing.

Ingredients for Cucumber Salad
- ½ cup of rice wine vinegar
- 1 tsp Sambal Oelek
- 1 Tbsp sugar
- 1 tsp of lemon zest
- 1 medium cucumber, thinly sliced
- 1 medium carrot, julienned
- ½ small red onion, thinly sliced
- About ½ cup radishes, thinly sliced
- ½ cup fresh cilantro, chopped
- ¼ cup of dry roasted peanuts, chopped (I used salted peanuts, so be mindful when adding salt)
- Salt and freshly ground pepper to taste

Directions

1. Whisk vinegar, sambal oelek, sugar, and lemon zest together in a bowl.
2. Add cucumber, carrot, radishes, and onion and toss.
3. Season it with salt and pepper. Cover and chill for at least 2 hours.
4. Drain excess liquid from the salad.
5. Top it with the cilantro and peanuts.

Mixed Smoked Vegetable Tray

Makes 1 party platter

This is a great recipe to use when you have a party coming up. You will even make vegetarians a fan of food smoking.

Ingredients
- 2 large sweet onions, cut into eighths
- 2 red bell peppers, cut into thin strips
- 2 yellow bell peppers, cut into thin strips
- 1 large cubano pepper, cut into thin strips
- 2 medium zucchini, cut into rounds about ¼-inch thick
- 4 medium red potatoes, skins on, cut into wedges
- 6 medium carrots, cut into long thick strips

Note: Try to get locally grown organic vegetables if possible

For Vinaigrette #1
- 1 cup extra virgin olive oil
- ½ cup good apple cider vinegar
- 3 tsp Dijon mustard
- ½ tsp kosher salt
- ¼ tsp freshly ground pepper

For Vinaigrette #2
- ½ cup extra virgin olive oil
- 1 Tbsp ground cumin
- 1 tsp Berbere (or substitute hot smoked paprika)
- ¼ tsp salt
- ¼ tsp freshly ground black pepper

Directions
1. You are going to smoke the carrots separately and the potatoes separately to allow for differing smoking times.
2. Mix together all of the ingredients of Vinaigrette #1.
3. Mix together all of the ingredients of Vinaigrette #2.
4. In a small glass casserole dish that will fit into your smoker, place the onions, all of the peppers, and the zucchini.
5. Pour about ½ cup of vinaigrette #1 over the vegetables and toss.
6. Place the potato wedges into another small glass casserole dish and pour the rest of vinaigrette #1 over the potatoes and toss.
7. In a third small glass casserole dish, place the carrots and toss with vinaigrette #2.
8. Smoke the mixed vegetables at 225°F for 1½ hours with Apple Bisquettes.
9. Smoke the carrots at 225°F for 2 hours with Apple Bisquettes.
10. Smoke the potatoes at 225°F for 2½ hours with Apple Bisquettes.

Mustard Smoked Rack of Lamb

Makes 2 servings

Lamb out of the Bradley Smoker is just phenomenal. Try this recipe, and you'll be amazed by the juiciness and tenderness of the smoked lamb.

Ingredients
- 1 rack organic pasture raised lamb (about 2½ lbs)

For Marinade
- 2 Tbsp good apple cider vinegar
- ¼ cup extra virgin olive oil
- 1 Tbsp horseradish
- 1 Tbsp mustard
- 1 Tbsp fresh rosemary
- 2 cloves garlic, rough chopped
- 1 tsp freshly ground black pepper

Directions
1. Mix all of the marinade ingredients and pour it into a large ziplock bag.
2. Put the rack of lamb into the bag, close it, and shake the bag to get all of the ribs covered with the marinade.
3. Put the bag into the refrigerator and marinate for 2 hours.
4. Remove the lamb from the bag, shake off the excess marinade.
5. Brush the entire lamb rack with the horseradish and mustard.
6. Place the lamb on an oiled smoker rack. Smoke at 220°F on Apple Bisquettes for 2–2½ hours, depending on desired doneness.
7. Remove lamb from the smoker and let it rest on a cutting board for 15 minutes.
8. Slice into single ribs and serve immediately.

Peaches Smoked with Brown Sugar and Bourbon

Makes 3–4 servings

This is a great dessert. Whether you have a sweet tooth or not, this smoked dessert will elevate your taste buds.

Ingredients
- 6 large peaches, cut in half and pitted
- 1 cup turbinado sugar (Sugar in the Raw)
- 1 cup good bourbon

Directions
1. Put the peach halves on an oiled smoker rack.
2. Into the pit hole, put some of the brown sugar and some of the bourbon.
3. Continue until all of the peach halves are filled with sugar and bourbon.
4. Smoke at 200°F for 2 hours with Apple Bisquettes.

Tip: These peaches are fantastic by themselves, or you can make your favorite shortbread recipe and make smoked peach shortcake topped with vanilla ice cream, whipped cream, or both!

Smoked Pickled Green Beans

Makes 2–4 servings

This is a great combination of smoking and pickling. A must try! These pickled green beans will keep in the refrigerator for at least six months. They are delicious in Bloody Marys, on cheese trays, with sandwiches, or just eaten from the jar.

Ingredients for Smoked Green Beans
- 1 quart good green beans
- 2 Tbsp extra virgin olive oil
- 1 tsp salt
- 1 tsp freshly ground pepper

Directions
1. Toss the beans in the extra virgin olive oil and salt and pepper in a glass baking dish.
2. Put the dish onto a rack in the smoker.
3. Smoke for 1 hour at 220°F. Apple Bisquettes give a nice flavor.
4. Cool the beans.
5. Mix vinegar, salt, and sugar until the salt and sugar dissolve.
6. Place the green beans and prepared pickling mixture in a 1 quart jar. Top off with more white vinegar if needed.

Ingredients for brine
- 2 cups water
- 1 cup white vinegar
- 3 tsp salt
- 1 tsp sugar
- 2 cloves garlic, peeled and halved
- ½ tsp mustard seeds

Directions
1. Bring water to a bowl in a medium saucepan.
2. Add vinegar, salt, sugar, garlic, and mustard seeds.
3. Stir until salt and sugar dissolve.
4. Place beans in 1-quart mason jar.
5. Pour hot brine over beans.
6. Screw on lid and let cool on counter (listen for the seal to pop).

Smoked Sea Scallops with Arugula Salad

Makes 2–3 servings

Sea scallops are a great product to smoke. The smoke penetrates the texture of the scallops nicely, which will give you that full smoky flavor.

Ingredients
- 1 dozen sea scallops, dry pack—if you live close to an ocean, buy local!

Note: Be sure to get dry pack scallops. Avoid the scallops in the milky liquid.

- 1 Tbsp salt
- 1 Tbsp freshly ground black pepper
- 1 lb bacon, thinly sliced

Directions
1. Remove the abductor muscle of the scallop.
2. Mix the salt and pepper together and pour it in a ziplock bag.
3. Add the scallops. Shake the bag to ensure that all the scallops get covered.
4. Remove the scallops from the bag and wrap each of them in a piece of the thinly sliced bacon.
5. Place all of the bacon-wrapped scallops on an oiled smoker rack.
6. Smoke the scallops at 210°F on Bradley Apple Bisquettes for approximately 45 minutes.

Ingredients for the Salad
- ⅓ cup good olive oil
- ⅓ cup sherry vinegar
- 1 Tbsp shallot, minced
- Salt and pepper
- 3 cups arugula

Directions
1. Combine shallot and vinegar.
2. Allow to sit for 15 minutes to mellow flavors.
3. Wisk in olive oil and add salt and pepper to taste.
4. Toss with arugula.
5. Plate salad and top with smoked scallops.

Smoked Silver Trout Spread

Makes 2 servings

This spread is great for a cocktail party or for an easy appetizer. And it's healthy!

Ingredients
- 2 whole silver trout, cleaned with heads on (or any fresh whole trout available in your area)
- Your choice of crackers, celery sticks, or baguette slices

For the Brine:
- ¼ cup kosher salt
- ¼ cup turbinado sugar (Sugar in the Raw)
- 1 quart water

Directions
1. Mix all the ingredients for the brine together. When all is mixed, spread the brine all over the trout.
2. Put the bag into the refrigerator for 24 hours.
3. Remove the trout from the bag and shake off any excess marinade.
4. Put the trout on a rack and let the fish dry for at least 1 hour.
5. Oil a smoker rack, put the trout on the rack, and smoke for 4 hours at 160°F on Alder Bisquettes.
6. When cooked, remove the trout. Pull the trout flesh off of the bone and flake it.

Ingredients for the Spread
- ½ cup mayonnaise
- ¼ cup prepared horseradish
- 1 Tbsp fresh lemon juice
- 3–4 dashes good hot sauce
- Salt and freshly ground pepper to taste

Directions
1. Mix all of the ingredients for the spread together with the flaked trout and refrigerate the mixture for at least 2 hours.
2. Serve with your choice of crackers, celery sticks, or baguette slices.

Smoked Stuffed Tomatoes

Makes 3–4 servings

This is a great dish to serve while entertaining your guests. It goes really well with toasted bread or crackers.

Ingredients
- 12 roma tomatoes, plum- or apricot-sized
- 1 cup good melting cheese, such as queso fresco or ricotta
- Freshly ground pepper and good sea salt
- chopped herbs of your choice
- crispy crackers or bread toasts
- sprig of parsley or cilantro

Directions
1. Core tomatoes and slice off the top using the small side of a melon baller.
2. Scoop out the innards—don't go too deep!
3. If the tomato won't stand, slice a very small slice off of the bottom of each tomato to make a flat surface.
4. Stuff each tomato with some of the cheese. The amount varies with the size of the tomato, but it's generally about a teaspoon.
5. Season with pepper. Use salt sparingly depending on the type of cheese you are using.
6. Oil the smoker rack and stand the stuffed tomatoes on the rack.
7. Smoke for 1½ hours at 240°F.
8. Remove the tomatoes, top with chopped herbs of your choice, and serve with crispy crackers or bread toasts and a sprig of parsley or cilantro for service.

Smoked Turkey Pastrami

Makes 4–6 servings

If you are a pastrami fan, you should definitely try this recipe. It's a fairly easy recipe when you are new to food smoking, but the taste is phenomenal.

Ingredients
- 3 –4 lbs of turkey breast
- 4 tsp cracked peppercorns
- 2 Tbsp coriander
- 4 tsp brown sugar
- 6 garlic cloves, minced
- 8 tsp sea salt
- 4 tsp sweet paprika
- 3 tsp mustard seeds
- 2 tsp ground ginger

Directions
1. Mix and pound all of the spices together. I used a large stone mortar and pestle.
2. Rub the spice mixture all over both sides of the turkey London broil.
3. Place the turkey in a glass casserole dish or large plate and cover with plastic wrap.
4. Refrigerate overnight then remove from the refrigerator and let it stand for 2 hours.
5. Rub the smoker rack with oil.
6. Preheat the smoker to 210°F using Apple Bisquettes.
7. Place the turkey on the oiled rack and smoke it, 3 hours for a 3-lb turkey London broil, until an instant thermometer reads 140°F.
8. Let the turkey rest for about 20 minutes.
9. For an authentic pastrami appearance, slice thin, in long pieces.

Serving Suggestion: This makes a delicious sandwich on rye bread. With a bit of butter, some good mustard, and perhaps some cole slaw, you will think "Pastrami."

Smoked Bluefish

Makes 6 servings

Smoked bluefish is delicious and ready for use in many dishes. For example, you can add it to a chowder as shown.

Ingredients
- One 2-lb fillet of bluefish (replaceable with mackerel)

For the Brine
- ¼ cup kosher salt
- ¼ cup turbinado sugar (Sugar in the Raw)
- ¼ cup organic soy sauce
- 4 fresh bay leaves
- 1 Tbsp black peppercorns
- 1 quart water

Directions
1. Mix brine ingredients well and pour into a large ziplock storage bag.
2. Add the fillet of bluefish into the ziplock, close it, and shake it around a little.
3. Brine in the refrigerator for 24 hours.
4. After 24 hours, remove the fish from the bag, shake off the excess brine, and put the fillet on a rack.
5. Let it dry for at least 1 hour.
6. Oil a smoker rack and put the bluefish on the rack.
7. Smoke for 4 hours at 160°F on Alder Bisquettes.

Smoked Cream of Tomato Soup

Makes 4 servings

We all know good old fashioned tomato soup. Adding a smoky twist gives your soup gourmet taste.

Ingredients
- 2 lbs medium-sized Roma tomatoes
- 1 cup extra virgin olive oil
- 1 Tbsp kosher salt
- 1 Tbsp freshly ground black pepper
- 2 cups unsalted chicken stock
- 1 cup heavy cream
- Salt and pepper to taste

Directions
1. Slice the Roma tomatoes in half lengthwise.
2. Set the tomatoes cut side up on an oiled smoker rack.
3. Sprinkle with the extra virgin olive oil, 1 Tbsp salt, and 1 Tbsp pepper.
4. Smoke at 220°F degrees for 1½ hours with Cherry Bisquettes.
5. Put the smoked tomatoes in a saucepan with the stock.
6. Bring to a boil, lower to a simmer, cover, and let the mixture simmer for about 30 minutes to break down the tomatoes.
7. When the tomatoes are soft and breaking down, use an immersion blender to liquefy the mixture. You can also use a blender if you divide it into batches.
8. When the mixture is almost totally liquid, add the cream and salt and pepper to taste.
9. Stir over low heat for 5 minutes and serve. Ideal with a grilled cheese sandwich made from three smoked cheeses (recipe on page 127).

Smoked Mussels with Zucchini Relish

Makes 2 servings

If you like mussels, you have to try them when they're smoked. Together with the zucchini relish, it will make your guests come back for seconds and even thirds!

Ingredients for Mussels
- 2 lbs mussels
- 1 cup white wine
- 1 cup water

Directions
1. Make sure the mussels are clean and debearded.
2. In a flat chef's pan, bring the white wine and water to a boil and add one layer of mussels.
3. When those mussels open, remove the mussels to a bowl and add another single layer of mussels.
4. Do this until you have steamed all of the mussels.
5. Remove all of the mussels from their shells and strain the steaming liquid through cheesecloth into a large bowl.
6. Sit the mussels in the strained liquid for about 30–40 minutes.
7. Put the mussels on an oiled rack and smoke at 150°F for 2½ hours with Apple Bisquettes.
8. Remove the mussels from the rack and put them on a platter to cool in the refrigerator. Serve with zucchini relish.

Ingredients for Zucchini Relish
- 1 lb zucchini, chopped
- ½ large onion, chopped
- ½ red bell pepper, chopped
- 1 clove garlic, minced
- 1 Tbsp kosher salt
- 1 cup sugar
- ¾ cup apple cider vinegar
- ¼ cup water
- 1½ tsp hot sauce
- ½ tsp turmeric
- ½ tsp mustard seeds
- ½ tsp celery seeds
- ½ tsp black pepper

Directions
1. Salt the zucchini, onion, pepper, and garlic in a colander and drain for about 2 hours.
2. Rinse and pat dry.
3. Combine the zucchini mixture and the rest of the ingredients in a pot and bring to a boil.
4. Boil for 20 to 30 minutes, until mixture is thickened and vegetables are softened.

Berbere Pork Belly for Dinner

Makes 3–4 servings

If you want to try something new and delicious, follow this recipe!

Ingredients
- 2½ lbs pork belly

For the Marinade
- ½ cup red wine (whatever kind you prefer—a Merlot works well)
- 8 sprigs fresh thyme
- 4 cloves garlic
- 1 Tbsp Dijon mustard
- 3 Tbsp extra virgin olive oil
- 1 Tbsp Berbere (or smoked hot paprika)
- 1 Tbsp freshly ground black pepper

Sauce for Service
- 2 Tbsp good white vinegar
- 1 cup red wine
- 1 Tbsp sugar
- 1 Tbsp Dijon mustard
- 2 tsp Berbere (or smoked hot paprika)
- 1 clove garlic, chopped
- 1 small shallot clove, chopped
- Salt and pepper to taste

Directions
1. Mix all the marinade ingredients together and add the pork belly. Marinate at least 24 hours.
2. After marinating, oil a smoker rack.
3. Remove the pork belly from the marinade.
4. Smoke the pork belly for 2 hours at 220°F and 2 more hours at 200°F. Alder Bisquettes provide a nice flavor to the pork.
5. Mix the ingredients for the sauce for service. Bring to a boil and then simmer for about 5 minutes.
6. Serve the sauce with the sliced pork belly.

Spicy Smoked Shrimp

Makes 2 servings

These shrimp are delicious as an appetizer. They are also delicious when combined with pasta or rice as a main course.

Ingredients
- 1 lb jumbo shrimp, shells on
- 3 Tbsp powdered garlic
- 3 Tbsp Cajun
- 1 Tbsp freshly ground black pepper
- 4 Tbsp organic soy sauce

Directions
1. Mix all of the above ingredients together in a ziplock bag.
2. Add the shrimp to the bag, refrigerate for 2 hours.
3. Place the shrimp on an oiled smoker rack.
4. Smoke at 190°F for 1 hour on Alder Bisquettes.

Tip: If you have good fresh shrimp, leaving the shells on will enhance the flavor. In fact, some people actually eat the shrimp with the shells. Either way, they will have a delicious and smoky flavor.

Three Smoked Cheeses

Makes 1 party platter

Smoking cheese is probably something you've heard of before. Follow the recipe, and you'll be able to make your own smoked cheese! Get the best, freshest cheeses that you can find. That will make a difference.

Ingredients
- 1 lb piece sharp provolone
- 1 lb braid of fresh mozzarella
- 1 lb piece of fontinella

Directions
1. Place each piece of cheese on a rack and let the cheeses sit at room temperature for at least 1 hour but ideally 3 hours.
2. Turn each piece of cheese a few times during the drying process.
3. Oil a smoker rack and smoke at 90°F for 1½ hours on Apple Bisquettes.

> **Tip:** The post-smoking treatment of the cheeses is important. The cheeses will have a beautiful color and aroma. It will be tempting to start slicing, but resist the temptation! Wrap each piece of cheese tightly in wax paper and store it in the back of your refrigerator for at least 2 days and more if you can wait a bit. When you do unwrap the cheeses, you will be glad you waited a few days.

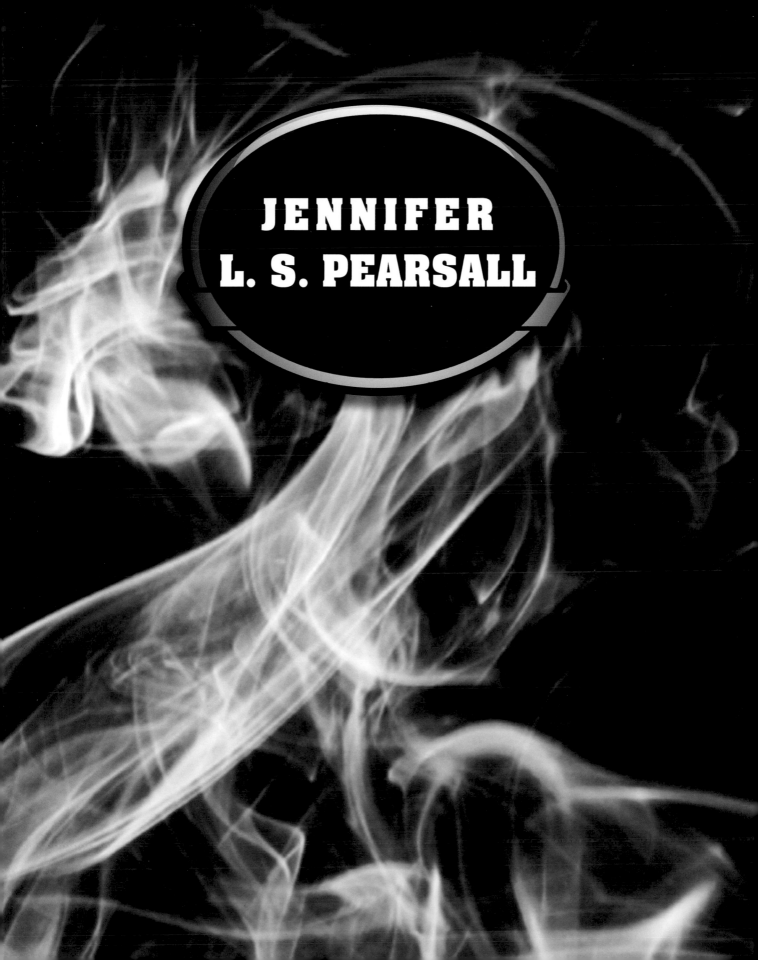

Smoked Apple Slaw and Pork Shoulder Sliders

Makes 6 sliders

My last smoked shoulder was a simple affair. I had guests in from out of town, and we wanted to take a day trip together. So, we decided to smoke a shoulder overnight and have it for dinner when we got home the next day. At dinner, I decided to slice it instead of shred it. But I still had a yen for a sandwich, and that's when I decided I needed to smoke something else to go with it: coleslaw.

Ingredients for Pork Shoulder
- ¾-lb jar rosemary and garlic brine (I used a brining mix from Williams-Sonoma)
- 2 lbs pork shoulder

Directions
1. Brine shoulder for 24 hours in a rosemary and garlic brining mix.
2. Put the shoulder in the smoker at 220°F, with Hickory Bisquettes during the first 2 hours. Let it smoke overnight for about 8½ hours. Early in the morning the next day, double foil-wrap it and let it go for 2½ hours more.
3. Remove and lay it to rest. Let it cool and slice.

Ingredients for Coleslaw
- 2 cups red and green cabbage, shredded and chopped
- ½ cup mayonnaise
- 2 Tbsp honey mustard salad dressing
- 1 Tbsp apple cider vinegar
- 2 medium apples (try honeycrisps or galas), cored and chopped
- 1 medium apple, cored and sliced into rounds
- Salt and pepper to taste
- 1 cup shredded carrots

Directions
1. Combine cabbage, carrots, and chopped apples in a large bowl.
2. Mix wet ingredients with a whisk or in a blender. This should be a lightly sauced and barely coated slaw mix. The cabbage, carrots, and apple will give off liquid as they smoke, and the fat in the mayonnaise will render, so avoid ending up with a warmly boiled slaw that does not absorb smoke.
3. Spread out a thin layer of slaw in a shallow aluminum roasting pan so the maximum surface area is exposed to the smoke.
4. Smoke at 215–220°F for about 2 hours. Use apple wood to complement with the apples in the slaw mix. The cabbage should be a bit less crisp but not limp, with brown toasting on the edges. Toss the mixture to redistribute.
5. Cut several slices of refrigerated smoked shoulder to fit slider-sized buns. Set naked in a hot pan until they sizzle and brown. Turn each piece and push to one side of the pan.

6. Lay in round apple slices to brown in the rendering fat. When all have color, remove the pan from heat.
7. Slice a slider roll in half. Spoon on smoked slaw and layer on the pork. Top off this juicy little sandwich with a browned apple slice. There should be ample slaw leftover on the side.

Tip: In slider form, these make great starters or sides for bigger barbecue and smoked meat meals, and they're super fare for football tailgating parties or autumn picnics.

Smoked Asian Burger

Makes 3 burger patties

In the summer of 2014, I moved from Wisconsin to Connecticut right in the middle of trying to put together my contribution to this cookbook. This is one of the recipes that came out of that move. This burger is like a Chinese food festival in your mouth.

Ingredients

- One 6–8-oz bag shredded broccoli slaw mix, raw, no sauce
- 1 lb ground round, 90/10 if you can get it
- 1 lb ground pork, unseasoned, 80/20 is preferable
- 3 Tbsp yellow curry sauce (Roland brand)
- 1 Tbsp low sodium soy sauce
- 1 Tbsp Chinese five spice mix
- 1 wedge Wasabi cheese if available (if not available, use wasabi sauce available in most grocery stores and white cheddar cheese)
- 2 cups panko breadcrumbs
- 3 Tbsp duck sauce, plus more for garnishing

Directions

1. Throw a bag of shredded broccoli slaw mix (a combination of broccoli, carrots, and cabbage) in the food processor. Pulse until vegetables are ⅓ of their original sizes. Do not let the food processor run on its own, or you'll end up with mush.
2. Combine chilled ground meats until evenly mixed. Incorporate processed vegetables, curry sauce, soy sauce, and Chinese five spice mix. The mixture should be wet enough that it cannot hold together as a patty.
3. Add panko crumbs to the meat mix a little at a time, combining to evenly distribute and absorb some wetness, but not so much that it becomes dry.
4. Divide meat mixture into 6 even portions, ⅓ lb each.
5. Using a sheet of wax paper, flatten 1 of the portions into a patty, spreading it out wider than you normally would for a bun. Do the same with another ⅓ lb portion.
6. Cut thin slices of wasabi cheese, or take a dollop of wasabi sauce and white cheddar cheese, and lay in the middle of 1 of the patties. If you like, add on 1–2 teaspoons of curry sauce or duck sauce. Keep everything centered on the patty, with plenty of meat framing it all around.
7. Take the other patty and top the one with the cheese. Slide your hand under the wax paper, cup the bottom patty to round up the meat edges, and pinch together with the edges of the top patty, sealing the cheese inside. Smooth ragged edges with your fingers. Repeat with remaining portions to make 3 burger patties.
8. Set each burger gently on a fine mesh rack. Smoke at 220°F with Hickory Bisquettes (a wood that complements bold flavors) for 1 hour and 30 minutes to 1 hour and 40 minutes. When the burger browns and glistens with juice, remove and cover with foil for 10 minutes.

To finish, I took a huge sesame seed hamburger bun, put a little bit of the leftover raw broccoli slaw blend on the bottom half, laid the rested burger on top, and poured on peanut sesame ginger sauce from Stonewall Kitchens, which is widely available and makes a large assortment of tasty sauces. The burger was wonderfully juicy, flavorful, and had just a little zing from the wasabi cheese.

Bacon-Wrapped Smoked Brown Sugar Onion Rings

Makes 10 rings

I am a potato girl, through and through. Fried, mashed, gratin, boiled, smashed, loaded, butter-only—you name it, there's nothing about a potato I don't love. Still, every once in a while I yearn for an onion ring to go with my next steak or burger.

Ingredients

- 2 large sweet onions, preferably Vidalia
- 1 lb regular sliced bacon
- ½ cup brown sugar

Directions

1. Chop off top and bottom of the onions and slice horizontally 3–4 times until you have a stack of equally thick rounds.
2. Punch out middle and center sections so you have 2–3 layers of each onion in a ring. Discard center knots or reserve for another dish.
3. Wrap a strip of bacon around each ring. Hold 1 end of a bacon strip against the onion, pinching them between your thumb and forefinger. Loop the long end through the center hole of the ring and back up around the outside, and keep repeating until you've wrapped the entire ring. Do not twist the bacon as you wrap; keep the flat of the bacon against the sides of the ring. The biggest rings take up to 1½ strips to wrap completely, while smaller rings require ½ a strip. Be careful not to snap smaller rings.
4. Roll onion rings in brown sugar, adding more as necessary. You want a light coating.
5. Space rings out evenly on your smoker's rack. Use Cherry Bisquettes since bacon can become bitter with heavy smoking. Smoke at 230°F for 2 hours, checking bacon doneness at the 90-minute mark and checking for a translucent color in onions.

I pulled mine off at the 2-hour mark because the bacon was cooked to my liking and found the rings perfectly done. The onions were tender with still a little density to them, like you'd have with perfectly cooked deep-fried onion rings. The sugared smoked bacon around them was just heavenly.

Smoked Buffalo Chicken Pot Pie

Makes 1 pie

I love the flavor of chicken wings. The problem is, I hate eating them. Most chicken wings have woefully little meat, and they are more often overcooked than not. That doesn't mean I don't get a craving for the little devils, and that craving gave rise to a better way to do this dish. I've recently switched to bone-in thighs for my smoking projects, as the meat is far more succulent after smoking than boneless thighs.

Ingredients
- 6–8 bone-in chicken thighs
- 3 cups hot wing sauce (Texas Pete or Archie Moore's Original)
- 8 oz shredded smoked white cheddar cheese (regular white cheddar will do but not orange cheddar)
- 1 cup celery, chopped
- ½ cup of green onions, chopped (whites and greens)
- 2 sheets puff pastry, thawed
- Crumbled blue cheese and extra hot wing sauce for garnish and dipping

Directions
1. Dress bone-in chicken thighs with 1 cup hot wing sauce in a bag. Massage the bag so thighs are evenly coated. Space out evenly on 2 racks in the smoker.
2. Over hickory (a stronger wood complements the buffalo sauce), smoke at 220°F for at least 2½ hours but no longer than 3. Since the chicken is going into the pie, being a smidge undercooked isn't a bad thing as it'll finish cooking inside.
3. Roll out 1 sheet of puff pastry to overlap the edges of the pie plate or a low-sided casserole dish. Line against the bottom of the dish and drape the excess over the sides. Prick the bottom several times with a fork and prebake in a 375°F oven for 15 minutes to get the pastry started.
4. While the bottom prebakes tear meat off the bone from smoked chicken thighs, discarding the skin, and put in a mixing bowl. You should have about 3 cups of meat.
5. Add chopped celery (leaves included) and chopped green onions to the chicken. Mix to distribute evenly. Add in shredded cheese and two cups of buffalo wing sauce. Toss to combine and pour into the shell of the prebaked pastry crust.
6. Roll out top crust, drape on top of the pie, and tuck the edges outside the bottom piecrust but inside the pie plate or casserole dish. Use fingertips or a carefully inserted butter knife to pull away the prebaked bottom crust from the side of the dish. You're making a pillow of a pie with the inside sealed completely within the pastry sheets.
7. Slash the top of the pie with a knife and stick it back in the oven still at 375°F. Set the timer for 45 minutes, take a look, and if needed give another 15 minutes for the crust to achieve the right color and the insides to bubble happily.

8. Remove from the oven and let sit for 10–15 minutes before serving with extra buffalo sauce for dipping. Crumble blue cheese over the top.

Add a cold beer plus a napkin for the corners of your mouth, and you may completely forget you ever had to use a carton of wet naps to eat your favorite wings.

Smoked Cream of Mushroom and Red Bell Pepper Soup

Makes 8–10 cups

Mushrooms fall into the same camp as Brussel sprouts, asparagus, and liver: you either love them or you hate them. If you love mushrooms, undoubtedly you will love cream of mushroom soup. This smoked version will make you love it even more.

Ingredients

- 4 pints of a variety of mushrooms, baby portabellas, white button, shitake
- 3 good-sized red bell peppers
- 1 sweet or yellow onion, diced
- One 24-oz box chicken stock
- 1 quart half-and-half
- ½ stick of butter
- 1 Tbsp cornstarch
- 1 cup milk
- salt and pepper to taste

Directions

1. Rinse and dry mushrooms. Trim off hard stem ends and dump mushrooms onto 1 of the mesh smoker trays.
2. Cut the peppers' stem ends and remove seed pods. Slice peppers in half and spread evenly on another smoker wire rack.
3. Use mild wood, such as Apple Bisquettes, for 90 minutes at 230°F. The mushrooms should shrink with their surfaces puckered—chewy, but still moist. Be careful not to dry them out.
4. Remove veggies and let cool in room temperature. Take half the mushrooms and chop coarsely. Julienne the peppers.
5. In a stockpot, add half the stock and all the diced onions.
6. Sweat the onion until the liquid disappears and the onion is translucent. Add the rest of the stock, mushrooms, and bell peppers. Bring to a simmer.
7. Slowly add half-and-half, stirring to combine. Lower the temperature, cock a lid on the pot, and let the soup think for 1–2 hours
8. When you're close to serving, mix the cornstarch with the cup of milk until dissolved and pour into the mixture, whisking as you go to combine. Raise the burner and stir frequently until the soup comes to a simmer. Replace lid and turn the flame to low. Salt and pepper to taste, stirring occasionally as the soup thickens before service.

Serve this with a chunk of peasant bread to sop up the dredges. This is a hearty, rich soup. The meatiness of the smoked mushrooms tells a tale of autumn, and the sweet smokiness of the red bell peppers is a lovely counterpoint that keeps this soup from being too heavy.

Smoked Greek Chicken Gyros

Makes 8–10 gyro wraps

Chicken, either roasted or smoked, is one of the great flavor platforms. All spices and fruits work with it. I recently smoked a boneless lamb shoulder I'd marinated in Greek yogurt and herbs, and I thought the chicken would serve equally well in making chicken gyros, a great backup when lamb is hard to find and also expensive.

Ingredients

- 1 whole chicken
- 2–3 cups of plain Greek yogurt
- 1½ tsp dried oregano
- 1½ tsp dried thyme
- 1½ tsp smoked paprika
- 1½ tsp salt
- 1½ tsp ground black pepper
- 1 Tbsp fresh garlic, finely crushed
- 2-3 cups seedless green grapes
- 1 cup fresh cilantro, chopped
- 1 cup bacon, chopped
- 1 bunch fresh iceberg, Romaine, or Boston lettuce leaves, chopped
- 8–10 pita or flatbread rounds, 6–8 inches in size

Directions

1. Remove gizzards and livers from the chicken.
2. Mix together 1½ cups of Greek yogurt, all dry spices, and crushed garlic. With your hand, lightly coat the entire chicken inside and out, sliding some under the skin without tearing it off.
3. Put the chicken into the smoker at 220°F over a mild wood, such as apple, for roughly 2½–3 hours.
4. As the first 40 minutes that the chicken has been in the smoker come to an end, pluck seedless grapes from stems and lay in a single layer in a low-sided aluminum roasting pan. Put in the smoker for the last dose of smoke and let them soft roast for another 40 minutes. Pull them out and set aside while the chicken finishes smoking.
5. Ascertain doneness with a pop-up timer or the look of the skin. The internal temperature should hit 165°F if you stick into the thickest part of the breast. Remove chicken from the smoker when done, tent with foil, and let sit for at least 20 minutes. When cooled, carve or hand tear meat into strips.
6. Prepare the roasted grape salad. Combine ½–1 cup of Greek yogurt (depending on how many you are serving) with smoked grapes, chopped cilantro, and chopped bacon. Mix until evenly combined.
7. Spread ¼ cup of grape salad on a round flatbread. Add chopped crisp lettuce and layer on strips of chicken.

Pair this with a tall glass of slightly sweet and minted iced tea, and you will have a wonderfully light dinner for an early summer evening.

Smoked Outside-In All-American Burger

Makes 3 large burgers

There is almost nothing better than the classic American burger—ketchup, yellow mustard, sweet relish, and gooey melted American cheese all on a soft, buttery, toasted bun. The only problem is that sometimes this becomes a slippery mess that just can't hold itself together. This recipe solves that messy problem. In fact, it made me realize that stuffing and smoking burgers should fast replace grilling a normal burger anytime. Done right, you will never have a dried-out, overdone burger. As for the addition of smoke, well, you know what that does to the flavor profile.

Ingredients

- 1 lb ground round, 90/10 if possible
- 1 lb ground pork, unseasoned, 80/20
- 6 slices of Kraft American cheese
- Ketchup
- Yellow mustard
- Sweet pickle relish
- 1 Tbsp Worcestershire sauce
- ¼–½ cup Heinz 57
- 2 cups garlic bread crumbs

Directions

1. Combine the two meats until homogenous, mixing in Worcestershire and Heinz 57 sauces as you go. The mixture should be wet, so it wouldn't hold together as a patty.
2. Add in garlic breadcrumbs a little at a time, stopping when it starts to come together but is still pliable. Do not add so much breading that the mixture becomes stiff.
3. Divide meat mixture into 6 even ⅓ lb portions. Place 1 portion on wax paper and form a patty a bit larger than your bun. Repeat with a second portion.
4. On the first patty, squirt a teaspoon each of ketchup and mustard in the center.
5. Fold a slice of American cheese in quarters so it's a neat square. Place on top of ketchup and mustard. Put a teaspoon of sweet relish on top of the cheese.
6. Place the second patty on top. Slide a hand under the wax paper and gently cup the lower patty, rounding up the edges as you do. With your other hand, pinch the edges of the 2 patties together, keeping the stuffing inside. Smooth the edges with your fingers so you have a rounded stuffed burger. Repeat with the remaining 4 meat portions.
7. Smoke with hickory, a moderate wood between mild and heavy, at 220°F for 90 minutes. The patties should be browned all over and glisten with juice. If you see pink on the surface, you haven't smoked it long enough. Check at the hour and give an extra 30 minutes if needed.
8. Remove patties carefully and top them with a bit more American cheese. Cover with foil and let rest for 10 minutes.
9. Toast your bun lightly, sandwich your burger, and serve.

Now all the things you usually put on a burger are inside, in part to keep it intact from first bite to last. Add whatever else you would like to your burger, but go easy on the bun slathering—except for cheese because there's really no such thing as too much cheese.

Smoked Pepper Relish

Makes 2–3 cups

After you've been smoking meat for a while, you begin to look at your smoker and wonder what else will work in this thing. Well, at least that's what I did one day. After that bit of wonderment struck me, I pawed my way through my refrigerator and spied a big bag of mini sweet peppers. I love mini sweet peppers. They are a little on the sweet side and go great on sandwiches or topped over steaks. Much like the smoker, smoking these sweet bell peppers is a matter of set it and forget it. My favorite thing to do with peppers is to make a relish out of them. Ninety minutes, one bag of mini sweet peppers, and a bit of olive oil. Who would have thought those three things plus your smoker could offer up so much?

Ingredients
- 32 oz uncooked sweet mini peppers
- Olive oil
- Salt and pepper

Directions
1. Cut off the tops of the peppers, halve, and seed them. You can also leave them to smoke whole.
2. Use Cherry Bisquettes during the first 40 minutes at 220°F or up to 250°F. Let them do their thing in the smoker for 90 minutes until tender.
3. Remove from the smoker. Put a handful at a time into a food processor, add olive oil (if you like it spicy, use a peppered oil or basil-enhanced olive oil), and pulse 3–5 times until it is reduced to a relish. Be careful not to puree. You want texture and uniform pieces.

Now, what can you do with this? It is one of my favorite things to put on a sandwich of roast chicken, and it adds some definite zing to a Philly cheesesteak, but it's also a great topping for meatloaf. Mixed with sour cream, it also makes a righteous baked potato topping. I'll also slather it over chicken thighs or breasts with diced onions and bake the cluck that way (the topping will caramelize as it cooks, adding even more dimension to the lovely sweet smokiness it already has), make pimiento cheese out of it (you get to back off the mayo some, thanks to the olive oil in the relish), top a burger with it, and mix it into a chicken salad spread.

Tip: If you want to turn your relish into a sauce, simply spin them more in your food processor or put them in a blender. Add that to a tomato sauce for pizza or pasta, and you have just elevated your dish to new flavor heights.

Smoked Pulled Pork, Wild Rice, and Cabbage Pie

Makes 1 pie

I've never heard anyone say "I'm sick of pulled pork," which makes me think we cook too little of this special creature. And the best part about too much pulled pork? Leftovers. If you're looking for something new to do with the last batch of leftover smoked pork shoulder you have on hand, try a crustless pie. You'll need pulled pork leftover from a shoulder or Boston butt you've previously smoked, but I'm not going to tell you how to smoke one. There are a hundred different ways to do that, and everyone has his or her own preference. The only thing I would suggest is that you don't use shoulder that's been slathered in sauce.

Ingredients

- 1½–2 cups smoked pulled pork (not with excess sweet or BBQ sauce)
- 3–4 cups Napa and Savoy cabbage, chopped and mixed
- 5 eggs
- ½ cup chicken stock
- ½ cup heavy cream
- ¼ cup sweet chili pepper relish (optional)
- 2 cups cooked wild rice
- 1 tsp each salt and pepper, plus to taste

Directions

1. Chop pulled pork into pieces. Add to a large mixing bowl.
2. Add cabbage and wild rice to the chopped pulled pork. Add sweet hot chili relish if you like an extra bit of zing. Toss to combine.
3. In a blender or bowl whisked by hand, combine eggs, cream, chicken broth, and a teaspoon each of salt and pepper. Beat until frothy.
4. Pour cabbage, pork, and rice mixture into a large dish. You'll need a deep dish pie plate or deep-sided casserole pan for this much material. Level across the top with a wooden spoon but do not pack down the mixture. It should be loose-sitting in the dish.
5. Slowly pour the egg mixture over the cabbage and pork mix from side to side. You want it to come just to the top of the mixture but not seep over the edge.
6. Place the dish in a 250°F smoker. If the pie surface is almost level with the top edge of your dish, place the dish on a jelly roll pan in case of a liquid bubble over. Smoke for 1 hour until the top is golden brown and it smells heavenly.
7. Check to see if the pie is done by inserting a dinner knife into the middle and pushing the filling aside. There should be no liquid when this pie is done. If you see liquid, put it back in the smoker in 15-minute increments until the same test shows it is dry and cooked through. If you need to extend your cooking time but the top is done, cover the dish with foil and put slits in it to let steam escape.

This is a filling dinner, but it isn't heavy. In the spring, a summer wheat beer would go really well with it. In the fall, a pleasant cabernet will be an excellent accompaniment.

Smoked Salmon Inverted Samosas

Makes 12 tartlets

I had committed to composing a recipe on smoked salmon after I moved to Connecticut and had a fresh supply available. I was going to do a galette, but the weekend this recipe was planned for ended up being quite warm, and I just didn't want to be in the kitchen with the stove running hot and long. When I secured a bag of tiny new potatoes and a carton of fresh pea shoots, I got an idea.

Ingredients

- ½ lb high quality salmon, skin on
- ¾ cup raw honey
- 1 Tbsp plus 1 teaspoon Vindaloo seasoning (available from Penzy's, Williams-Sonoma, and ethnic food asiles in grocery stores)
- 8 oz mascarpone

- 1 cup whole milk
- 2 cups pea shoots, 1 cup whole and 1 cup chopped
- 12 small baby potatoes
- 8 sheets filo dough
- 4 round lemon slices
- Butter to roughly coat filo dough

Directions

1. Set a smoking rack over a cutting board and lay 4 round lemon slices as feet for the salmon. Set the salmon filet skin side down on the lemons.
2. In a microwave, melt half of the raw honey. Add 1 teaspoon of Vindaloo spice and mix. When the honey is cool enough, rub it over the top and sides of the salmon.
3. Preheat the smoker to 220°F as salmon takes a short time to smoke. As soon as you set the salmon inside the smoker, use Apple Bisquettes and leave for 1 hour until perfectly cooked and moist. The salmon will get a follow-up in the oven, so don't overdo it in the smoker.
4. Meanwhile, quarter the potatoes and boil until tender. Chill them in an ice bath to stop the cooking. Drain and set aside.
5. Butter or oil a muffin tin. Cut the filo dough sheets into smaller squares to fit in each muffin tin cup. Place 4 stacked filo dough sheets into each cup. Swab the top sheet and edges of the filo dough with butter.
6. In a saucepan over low heat, melt the remaining raw honey, add a tablespoon of Vindaloo seasoning, a cup of milk, and a pinch of salt. Add mascarpone once honey is melted. Stir until sauce is smooth. Remove pot from burner and let the sauce thicken while you prepare the tartlets.
7. Place 4 potato quarters at the bottom of each filo cup. Add a tablespoon of chopped pea shoots on top. Pour a tablespoon of sauce over the pea shoots and potatoes. Top with a hunk of salmon and add another tablespoon of the remaining sauce.
8. Pop into a preheated 350°F oven until the filo starts to tan, about 40 minutes. The tart components should be bubbling. You can hit the broiler for a minute to finish coloring the filo golden.

Serve once they're cool enough to remove from the muffin tin (a butter knife inserted carefully between the filo and the tin will help lift these out), and enjoy these flavorful treats either by themselves or complemented with sour creamed and dilled cucumbers on the side.

Smoked Sausage and Mozzarella Bites

Makes 30 meatballs

Good sausage, fresh mozzarella, and a zesty, tangy marinara sauce are a simple yet heavenly combination. When you're able to add smoke to the mix, you end up with something downright addictive. Easy to make, these nifty little appetizers can be made ahead of time in a big batch, frozen while raw, thawed in a short time, and ready for a short siesta in the smoker before an evening dinner of other Italian fare.

Ingredients
- One 8-oz container of mozzarella pearls (Belgioioso)
- 1–1½ lbs of sweet Italian sausage (I used Johnsonville)
- ½ lb plain ground pork
- 1 jar marinara sauce

Directions
1. If your sausage is in links, slit the casings along the length of the links and remove sausage meat underneath it. Mix plain ground pork with the sausage meat and chill in the refrigerator for 1 hour, since colder and firmer meat is easier to work with. Plain ground pork ups the fat content in the meat mixture, preventing it from drying out during smoking.
2. Roll a tablespoon of meat mixture into a ball. Flatten out the meatball with your palm.
3. Place a pearl of mozzarella in the center of the patty. Bring the sides of the meat up around the cheese to gather at the top. Pinch off excess meat and roll between your palms to make a round meatball between the size of a shooter marble and a large gumball. You don't want so much meat that you don't taste the mozzarella inside but you also don't want so little meat that cheese oozes out during smoking.
4. Lay parchment paper on the jerky tray and place meatballs on it evenly spaced. Two trays can accommodate 30 meatballs. In the smoker, use Cherry Bisquettes, though apple or any softer, sweeter woods also work, and smoke at 225°F. Check at 90 minutes with smoke for the first hour. Remove the racks after 2 hours when the meatballs are nicely browned.
5. Remove finished appetizers and cover with foil while you warm up a jar of marinara sauce. Five minutes later, skewer meatballs with an appetizer fork and dip in marinara.

Tip: Instead of using sausage meat, you can use fresh ground pork from scratch with your own seasonings. Try to find pork that's the same 80/20 meat/fat ratio as most ground beef. Ground pork with a heavier fat content oozes too much liquid as it cooks, making a mess of your smoker

Smoked Spiced Pork Tenderloin with Smoked Plum Sauce

Makes 4 servings

I'm going to call this recipe accidental genius. I was planning to stuff and smoke a pork tenderloin with apples, pears, and a lovely honeyed goat cheese. But somewhere between taking the tenderloin out of the butcher paper and butterflying it, I forgot what I was doing. I had a bunch of Tex-Mex spices sitting on the work table, ready for another recipe. The next thing I know I'm mixing up a dry rub of the spices for the tenderloin, and the rest is history.

Ingredients
- ¼ cup brown sugar
- 1½ tsp cayenne pepper
- 1½ tsp onion powder
- 3-lb pork tenderloin
- 8 plums, halved and pitted
- 2 cups pea shoots (as garnish)
- 5 oz honeyed goat cheese
- Salt and pepper to taste

Directions
1. Mix a dry rub of half the quantities of brown sugar and cayenne, onion powder, and pepper and salt to taste.
2. Prepare the tenderloin at uniform thickness, slicing off edges if necessary. Rub down the tenderloin inside and out.
3. Roll and tie it up into a package. Smoke with Cherry Bisquettes at 220°F for 5 hours. At the top of hour 5, double foil wrap it and let it go another 2 hours.
4. Place the plums flesh side up in a low-sided aluminum roasting pan. Sprinkle with brown sugar and cayenne pepper.
5. Smoke the plums at 220°F for 90 minutes with Cherry Bisquettes. They should render down nicely into a gorgeous purple syrup. Remove to cool.
6. Pour plums (including the skins) and their syrup into a food processor and churn until they form a smooth puree.
7. Heat the puree in a small saucepan over a medium flame. Taste and flavor with more brown sugar if still tart. Let it come to a summer.
8. For service, quickly sear slices of the tenderloin to add a little caramel color to them. Lay them on a bed of fresh pea shoots and ladle on the warm plum sauce. Crumble on a bit of soft honeyed goat cheese.

The sweet and spicy plum sauce, backed by its hint of smoke, played perfectly with the spiced pork tenderloin, while the creamy, sweet cheese added an almost heavenly contrast of texture and flavor. Oh, and those pea shoots? Frankly, I intended to use them decoratively, but they were so good on the fork with the pork, plum, and cheese that I highly recommend you use them, too.

Smoked Stuffed Italian Burger

Makes 1 burger patty

I like stuffing burgers. If you do it right, it lets you get a whole lot of different flavors without having burger toppings sliding all over the place. This burger was one of my first attempts at stuffing, and I have to admit, I got a little out of hand with both the stuffing and the meat. In the end, I'd used about a full pound of ground meat and created a true gut-buster no bun could handle, hence my lack of bun in this recipe. If you wish to make a burger patty small enough to fit a bun, cut your meat back by at least a third and use a small tomato.

Ingredients
- ½ lb lean ground pork
- ½ lb ground veal
- 3 Tbsp pesto
- 1 thick slice of tomato
- Several slices of smoked provolone
- 1 tsp each salt and pepper, plus more to taste

Directions
1. Combine ground meats with 2 tablespoons of pesto and a teaspoon each of salt and ground black pepper. Divide the mixture in 2.
2. Tear off 2 large sheets of wax paper and lay 1 on a flat work surface.
3. Form one of the 2 meat mixture halves into a firmly packed ball and set it in the middle of the wax paper. Place the other sheet of wax paper over the top and press down with your hand to flatten. Using a rolling pin, widen the patty out into a large round big enough so there's a ½ inch of meat around the circumference of the tomato slice set in the middle of the patty.
4. Slide your hand under the waxed paper of the finished patty, flip the patty onto a cutting board, and peel the wax paper off. Reuse to form a second identical patty with the remaining meat mixture.
5. Place rectangular slices of smoked provolone cheese on the first patty. Spoon a generous tablespoon of pesto on top of the cheese then lay on the tomato slice.
6. Flip your second patty gently on top of the stack and peel back the wax paper. Be careful not to break up the patty. Gently pinch the sides of the 2 patties together, sealing in the cheese, pesto, and tomato. Seal tightly against the ingredients inside so there won't be any leaks during the cooking process.
7. Smoke at 220°F using Cherry Bisquettes for about 1 hour and 45 minutes. My burger had good color on the outside and it didn't look dry at all at 90 minutes, so I threw some extra provolone across the top and let it smoke for another 15 minutes. When cooked, remove and tent with foil to cool.

I chose to eat my burger patty with pasta. You can boil some spaghetti and toss it hot with leftover pesto and the unused tomato. Serve on a dinner plate and set the burger on top. Slice it in half, and let the beautiful smoky juices run out.

Smoked Summer Chowder

Makes 8–10 cups

In Connecticut during late August, my grocery stores stock a dizzying array of tomatoes. Paired next to the giant bins of local sweet corn, the two are an irresistible combination. After one of my pilgrimages to a circuit of markets, I thought a summer chowder was in order. I suggest using as many varieties of tomatoes as you can, as they run the gamut in acidity, sweetness, tartness, and texture, offering a complexity to this dish you couldn't get with just one variety.

Ingredients

- 1 pint multicolored cherry tomatoes
- 2 yellow on-the-vine tomatoes
- 1 beefsteak tomato
- 2 kumato tomatoes
- 2 red on-the-vine tomatoes
- 4 ears of corn
- 4 bone-in skinless chicken thighs
- One 24-oz box of chicken stock
- 1 can evaporated milk
- 1 cup heavy cream
- 2 Tbsp Val Verde spice rub
- 2 tsp fine sea salt
- ¼ cup all-purpose flour
- 4 medium yellow potatoes
- ½ cup bacon fat
- Croutons to serve

Directions

1. Leave the cherry tomatoes whole and quarter the bigger varieties. Lay in a single layer on a fine meshed jerky rack. Put an aluminum roasting pan under the rack to catch the juices. Smoke for 1½ hours at 220°F with Apple Bisquettes.
2. Pull back the husks of the corn and remove the silk. Fold the husks back around the corn and soak cobs in cold water for 2–3 hours. Drain and blot dry.
3. Soften bacon fat in the microwave for a few seconds. Mix in a teaspoon of sea salt and a tablespoon of Val Verde spice rub.
4. With a pastry brush, swab each cob with the bacon fat and spice mixture, then gather husks back around. Space evenly across 2 shelves in your smoker using the same wood you used for the tomatoes. Smoke for 1½ hours at 220°F.
5. Rub chicken thighs with sea salt and Val Verde spice rub to lightly coat. Smoke for 2½–3 hours with the same wood. Do not overcook—the chicken should be glistening, tender, and pull off the bone easily. Set aside to cool.

To Assemble the Soup

1. Pour tomatoes and their juices leftover from the smoke into a stock pot and add in chicken stock. Bring to a simmer over a medium flame.
2. As stock simmers, tear the chicken thigh meat from the bone into even pieces. Add to the stock.
3. Peel back the husks of each smoked cob and chop off the base so you can stand the corn on a flat, level base. Run the knife down the sides of the cob to remove the kernels. Four cobs should yield 2 or more cups of corn. Add to the pot and raise flame to medium high.

4. Peel and dice potatoes into ¾-inch pieces. Add to the pot and bring to a gentle boil for 5–7 minutes. Lower to a simmer and lid, stirring from time to time, until potatoes are tender. Add in a can of evaporated milk.
5. Whisk heavy cream into the flour until smooth or mix in a blender. Add to the pot and stir to combine.
6. Let the chowder work for 4 hours. I transferred my soup to a slow cooker because I don't like leaving gas stoves unattended. Stir every hour or so and add more Val Verde spice rub and salt as needed to flavor.
7. If you have the time, let it sit overnight in the refrigerator. Reheat it the next day and serve with garlic and butter croutons on the top.

I'm a firm believer in soups taking 24 hours to really become the greatness they're intended to be. Unless you've got an ingredient that's going to disintegrate with this kind of cooking, there's simply no better meld of flavors and richness when you let a soup sit and cook.

Tip: Bone-in chicken thighs are much juicier than boneless thighs, and it is only a minor hassle of removing the chicken off the bone when you're done smoking.

Smoked Onion and Bacon Jam

Makes 2 cups

This concoction, like smoked sweet pepper relish, is really an example of how simple is sometimes better. Other than onions, bacon, and a little brown sugar, all you need is a little time. Since this nice little topping can be put on almost anything—biscuits, steaks, grilled cheese sandwiches, mac-n-cheese, roast chicken sandwich wraps—I usually make up a pretty large batch.

Ingredients

- 1 lb regular cut bacon
- 3 large sweet onions
- 1 Tbsp olive oil
- ½ cup light brown sugar
- Salt and pepper to taste

Directions

1. Slice off tops and bottoms of the onions and remove the tough outer layer. Quarter to create large sickle-moon onions.
2. Put onion slices in a gallon-sized ziplock freezer bag. Add olive oil and lightly salt and pepper. Massage the bag so all the onions are coated.
3. Pour lubricated onions on a rack and smoke them at 230–240°F for 90–120 minutes with Apple Bisquettes at the start. Onions can get bitter in smoke, so go easy with the smoke and err on the side of caution. The onions should become translucent with a brown tinge.
4. When done, set the onions aside to cool. Slice a pound of bacon into 1-inch squares (hint: chilled bacon is easier to slice).
5. Warm a deep-sided sauce pan to medium high and add the bacon pieces. Stir now and again until they start to brown. Remove and place on a paper-toweled plate to soak up excess oil. Pour most of the rendered bacon fat into a heatproof container for use later, but leave a little in the pan.
6. Add smoked onions to the pan. Stir until a medium-brown color (be careful not to burn), then add in brown sugar. Stir over a low flame, letting onions absorb the sugar and fat without burning. When you've got a lovely mess of smoked onions and sugar in a thick, darkening, jam-like state, add back bacon and raise the flame slightly. Taste, add more sugar if you need, and lower the flame to keep steaming. Keep stirring to prevent sticking and burning until ready to serve.

I tend to put this on steaks as a topping. But the night I whipped up this batch of jam for the book, I had some gorgeous Portobello mushroom caps on hand. Just as I laid the steaks on the hot grill, I filled 2 mushroom caps with a generous helping of the smoked onion and bacon jam, then crumbled a bit of tangy blue cheese on top. I placed the mushrooms to the side of the hot grill (indirect flame), and by the time the steaks were off and had rested for about 7 or so minutes, the mushrooms were cooked through, the jam had developed a dark lacquer, and the blue cheese had melted nicely and browned.

BRADLEY SMOKER TIPS AND TRICKS

- Typically, you smoke half of your total cooking time.

- Smoke absorbs better when the meat is still raw, so the meat will absorb most of that good smoky flavor during the beginning of your smoking process.

- When wood is allowed to burn from charcoal to ash, the wood will release its tars and resins, creating a bitter aftertaste that lingers on smoked foods. The Bradley Smoker system extinguishes the wood before it burns to ash. The results are clearly noticed in the taste.

- To remove your food easily from the racks when your meal is ready, we would recommend using nonstick spray on the racks or, even better, use the Bradley Smoker Magic Mats.

- If you want to use foil or a pan in your Bradley Smoker, don't cover the entire rack. It will trap heat and smoke in the bottom half of your smoker, creating inconsistent cooking conditions.

- Good things come to those who wait. Food smoking is all about low and slow: low temperature and a slow process. Give the smoke the time to cascade over your food for that great smoky flavor.

- Don't close the damper expect for when it's windy. Condensation will build up, and it won't necessarily make your food taste better.

- Resist the temptation to constantly open the door to check on your food. Bradley Smokers are designed so you can sit back and relax while your smoker does all the work. Make sure you have a good meat thermometer, then you only have to check every hour or so.

- The reason why Bradley Smokers do not have a glass door:

  - While smoking food, you do not see anything through the glass since your Bradley Smoker is filled up with fragrant smoke.

  - After using a smoker with a glass door a few times, the glass will be blackened, requiring regular cleaning.

  - The doors on the Bradley Smokers are designed so the tower is completely insulated to keep in heat and smoke. Glass is a poor insulator, creating heat-loss, and it will become too hot to handle.

ACCESSORIES

& 6 Rack Weather Guards

dley Digital Smokers (2-rack, 4-rack,
and Original Bradley Smoker.

king on hot days proved to be quite
Smoke Adaptor attaches between the
xible aluminum tube that allows the
ur food, enabling you to do a true cold
ack smokers.

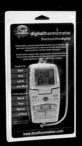

Digital Thermometer

Compact and battery-powered, this
programmable unit makes it easy
to select the type of meat, cooking
preference and accurate internal
temperature. Take the guesswork out
of roasting and smoking temperatures
and make it perfect every time!

Four Jerky Racks

Non-stick Jerky Racks prevent jerky
from sticking. The smaller mesh on
jerky racks makes them ideal for
smoking items like oysters, nuts,
vegetables and sausages.

Bradley Recipe Collection Vol. 1

Our most popular recipe collection
featuring: meat, fish, seafood,
cheese, fruit, nuts & more, in a
handy fantail format. 56 recipes.

laple Syrup,
organic and
at to use as a
rinade, part
g process, or
its own!

FLAVOR BY BRADLEY

Award Winning Food Smoking Technology

BRADLEYSMOKER.COM